HULLABALOO!

BELFAST

Edited by Allison Dowse

First published in Great Britain in 2003 by
YOUNG WRITERS
Remus House,
Coltsfoot Drive,
Peterborough, PE2 9JX
Telephone (01733) 890066

All Rights Reserved

Copyright Contributors 2003

SB ISBN 1 84460 234 6

FOREWORD

Young Writers was established in 1991 as a foundation for promoting the reading and writing of poetry amongst children and young adults. Today it continues this quest and proceeds to nurture and guide the writing talents of today's youth.

From this year's competition Young Writers is proud to present a showcase of the best poetic talent from across the UK. Each hand-picked poem has been carefully chosen from over 66,000 'Hullabaloo!' entries to be published in this, our eleventh primary school series.

This year in particular we have been wholeheartedly impressed with the quality of entries received. The thought, effort, imagination and hard work put into each poem impressed us all and once again the task of editing was a difficult but enjoyable experience.

We hope you are as pleased as we are with the final selection and that you and your family will continue to be entertained with *Hullabaloo! Belfast* for many years to come.

Contents

Beechfield JMI & N School
Aidan Stewart (9)	1
Hayley Hawkes (9)	1
Samantha McClure (9)	2
Nicola Stewart (8)	2
Naomi Whyte (8)	3
Rebecca Wilson (9)	3

Botanic Primary School
Bhargavi Chandrasekar (11)	4
Neil McAllister (11)	4
Emma Mitchell (11)	5
Michelle Veighey (10)	6
Andrew Hanratty-Mullan (9)	6
Aifric Smyth (10)	7
Fiona Butler (9)	7
Ciaran Bowen (9)	8
Molly Davey (10)	8
Daniel Kerr (10)	9

Carryduff Primary School
Jason Magill (11)	9
Benjamin McNeely (11)	10
Matthew Gibson (11)	10
Simon Brown (11)	11
Kerry Gilmore (11)	12
Ben McGirr (11)	12
Danielle Clifton (11)	13
Danielle Neill (11)	14
Rebekah McClean (10)	14
Hannah McCaughan (11)	15

Glenwood Primary School
Tommy Burns (11)	15
Christopher Hill (11)	16
Melissa Johnston (11)	17

Curtis Mawhinney (11)	17
Jason Beasant (11)	18
Nikki Smith (11)	18
Dean Murphy (11)	19
David Crane (11)	19
Samantha Seaton (10)	20
David Hussain (11)	20
Brooke Goodwill (10)	21
Ryan Azzabi (11)	21
Ellen Hill (11)	22
Lisa McCaw (11)	22
Jason Barrow (10)	23
Claire Wilson (10)	23
Nicholas Wilson (10)	24
Marcus Kane (11)	24

Holy Rosary Primary School

Louise McLaughlin (9)	25
Sarah Montgomery (9)	26
Laura Curry (9)	26
Bebhinn Schaible (9)	26
Ciaran Fitzpatrick (10)	27
Conall Bailie (10)	27
Aaron Black (10)	28
Paul Stelges (10)	28

Lough View Integrated Primary School

Aoife Rose O'Reilly (10)	29
Selina Lewis (10)	29
Amie Martin (11)	30
Emma Osborne (11)	30
Maeve McQuillan (11)	31
Conor Locke (10)	32

Malvern Primary School

Jenny Clements (11)	32
Demi Sanlon (8)	33
Naomi Wilson (8)	33

Ashleigh Gaynor (8)	33
Billy Boomer (10)	34
Alan Montgomery (8)	34
Elizabeth Mawhinney (10)	35
Philip Morrison (8)	36
Shannon Brownlee (8)	36
Natasha Johnston (9)	37
Rebecca Verner (8)	37
Colin Johnston (11)	38
Karl Harper (9)	38

Mersey Street Primary School

Christina Keenan (9)	39
Christopher Leebody (10)	39
Megan Todd (9)	40
Chelsea Charlesworth (10)	40
Jade Morrow (11)	41

Our Lady of Lourdes Primary School

Niamh McCusker (8)	41
Ciara Lynch (9)	42
Georgia Behan-Doyle (9)	42
Gareth McCrellis (8)	43
Christopher Gormley (8)	43
Nathan Kelly (9)	44
Megan McCarthy (8)	45
Eimear Rosato (8)	46
Naomh Rimes (8)	46
Megan Reid (9)	47
Toyah Warnock (8)	48
Sean Loughran (9)	48
Kilian Gargan (9)	49
Grace Prenter (9)	49
Claudia McCracken (9)	50
Matthew Deighan (8)	50
Declan Coghlan (9)	51
Dermot Trainor (9)	51
Conor Marley (8)	52

Sophie Magee (9)	53
Rory Millar (8)	54
Larragh Mann (9)	55
Rachel Bannon (9)	56
Clare Burns (8)	57
Claire Doyle (8)	58
Conor McLarnon (9)	59

Rosetta Primary School

Jessica Barrett (11)	59
Amanda Herron (11)	60
Amy Harrison (10)	60
David Moutray (12)	61
Laura Gibson (11)	61
Kirsten Dodsworth (11)	62
Adam Campbell (11)	62
Matthew Weir (10)	63
Stephen Craig (10)	63
Susan Burrell (10)	64
Rebecca Shaw (11)	64
Alannah Scott (11)	65
Shannon Ferguson (10)	65
Alan Foster (11)	66
Catherine Magill (10)	66
Claire McCaul (11)	67
Christina Elliott (11)	68

St Bernadette's Primary School

Hannah Barnes (8)	68
Una Beales (9)	69
Emma Bonner (9)	69
Joanne Savage (11)	70
Lorraine Loughran (8)	70
Nicole Bradley (10)	70
Carla Butler (9)	71
Joleen Clarke (11)	71
Alison Curley (11)	72
Nikita McMullan (11)	72

Fiona Hall (11) 73
Roisin Carey & Caitlin Corbett (11) 73

St Bride's Primary School
Jack McCambridge (10) 74
Emily Kate Herbert (10) 74
Adam Valente (10) 75
Jéri Cronin (11) 75
Katie McMullan (10) 76
Nicola Quinn (10) 77
Eavan Prenter (10) 78
Marie Louise Farag (10) 79
Ronan McDaid (11) 79
Oliver Tumelty (10) 80
Katie Connolly (10) 80
Michael McAuley (10) 81
Claire Whittley (10) 81
Helen Quinn (10) 82
Elspeth Vischer (10) 83
Rebecca Campbell (10) 84
Ciara McFerran (10) 85
Rebecca Copeland (11) 85
Bronagh Macartney (11) 86
Connor McMurray (10) 86
Christian Boyle (10) 87
Denis McKaigue (11) 87
Zara O'Reilly (10) 88
Charlotte Doran (10) 88
Rachael McKinney (10) 89
Sarah Niblock (11) 89
Lorcan Gallagher (11) 90
Daniel McCrea (11) 90
Aoife Leonard (11) 91
Niamh O'Hare (11) 91
Orla Campbell (11) 92
Laurence Magowan (11) 92
Una Grace (11) 93
Maria Martin (11) 94

Anastasia McBride (11)	94
Sarah McSparron (11)	95
James Trainor (11)	95
Caroline McElroy (11)	96
Owen Farnan (11)	96
Olivia Lucas (11)	97
Kevin Shannon (11)	98
Conn McGrath (11)	98
Maeve McMullan (11)	99
Caoimhe Sheppard (11)	99
Catherine Macaulay (11)	100
Emma Beattie (11)	100
Beth Gilmore (11)	101
Ross Whittley (11)	101
Christine Gallen (11)	102
Joe Begley (11)	103
Daniel Nolan (11)	103
Jane Mulholland (11)	104
Stephanie Donald (10)	104
Thomas Southern (11)	105
Aoife Carberry (11)	106
Rose McKeogh (10)	106
Jenny Putt (11)	107
Alexandra Gilroy (10)	107
Laura Boyle (11)	108
Peter McAuley (10)	108
Clare Toner (10)	109
James Rooney (10)	109
Máire Toner (10)	110
Aoife Corrigan (10)	110
Donal Keenan (10)	111
Niamh Muldoon (10)	111
Laura Lee (10)	112
Christopher Kinney (10)	113
Benjamin Lee (10)	113
Ruaidhri Austin (10)	114
Michael Webb (10)	114
Ronan Cullen (10)	115

Kevin Martin (10)	115
Anna Kerr (10)	116
Emma Johnson (10)	117
Eoin Kelly (10)	118
Nadine Quinn (10)	118
Muhadasaeh Suhail (10)	119
Catherine Blaney (10)	119
Marie Finnegan (10)	120
Brendan Ferguson (10)	120
Katie Clarke (10)	121
Patrick Fee (10)	121
Jennifer Wright (10)	122
Aoibhe McCann (10)	123
Kevin Scott (10)	123
Candice Robinson (10)	124
Mary Carson (8)	125
Gavin McGranaghan (8)	125
Stephen McKeever (8)	126
Donal Prenter (8)	127
Tom Dowling (8)	127
Amy Doran (8)	128
Charley Morrison (8)	128
Conall Cahill (8)	129
James Gildea (8)	129
Jane Kelly (8)	130
Michael Loughrey (8)	130
Lara Smyth (9)	131
Sophie Trainor (8)	131
Lianna Dalmeny (9)	132
Nicholas Ferguson (8)	132
John O'Neill (9)	133
Finn McKenna (9)	133
Orla Herity (9)	134
Jack McCann (9)	134
Fiona Hunt (9)	135
Rebecca Carr (9)	135
Olivia McCauley (9)	136
Nainsi McKernan (9)	136

Beulah McGeachie (9)	137
Anna Maguire (9)	137
Megan O'Hare (9)	138
Melissa Timoney (9)	138
Emma Quinn (9)	139
Rachel Connolly (9)	139
Patrick Short (9)	140
Colette Duffy (9)	140
Kate O'Hara (9)	141
Tony Stow (9)	141
Mary Kervick (8)	142
Lauren McLaughlin (9)	142
Orla Gormley (8)	143
Mark Salters (9)	143
Jade Zemrowsky (9)	144
John Kerr (9)	144
Conor McGowan (9)	145
Ben Leonard (9)	145
Eimear McDonnell (9)	146
Ruairi Fallon McGuigan (9)	146
Sorcha Foster (9)	147
Aedin O'Kane (9)	148
Alice Keenan (10)	148
Rory Flanagan (9)	149
Katherine O'Boyle (9)	149
Méabh McHugh-Hill (9)	150
Ben Johnston (10)	150
Garrett Cullen (9)	151
Ellen Gordon (9)	151
Beth McMullan (9)	152
Lucy Southern (10)	153
Sarah McLernon (9)	153
Paula Moloney (9)	154
Joshua O'Hagan (9)	155
Caelan Rush (9)	155
Conall Forker (9)	156
Iswarya Kalyan (9)	156
Matt McClean (9)	157

Chloe MacAuley (10)	157
Katie Campbell (9)	158
Odhran Burke (9)	159
Ellen McGrath (9)	160
Aoife Montague (10)	160
Rachael Rainey (9)	161

St John The Baptist Boys' Primary School

Conor Donnelly (8)	161
Liam Williams (10)	162
Aiden Cochrane (8)	162
Conor Nugent (11)	163
Mark McKenna (9)	163
Conor Willoughby (11)	164
Mark McCaffrey (8)	164
Carlo Angelone (11)	165
Conal Sheppard (8)	165
Matthew McPolin (11)	166
Eamann McDowell (8)	166
Kevin Shannon (9)	167
Ryan Willoughby (9)	167
Ryan Sewell (9)	168
Niall Connolly (8)	168
Colum Carroll (11)	169
Davin Clarke (11)	170
Jackson McGreevy (8)	170
Michael Duffin (9)	171
Michael Maxwell (9)	171
Ryan McBride (8)	172
Paul McCann (8)	172
Gary Crossan (9)	173
Peter Forde (10)	173
Brendan Clarke (9)	174
Brendan McCann (9)	174
Ryan Clarke (9)	175
Gavin Savage (9)	175
Kurtis McGreevy (10)	176
Luke Boyle (9)	176

Luke Clarke (9)	177
Eoin Morgan (10)	177
Christopher McGuigan (9)	178
Aidan Scott (9)	178
Matthew Mallon (8)	179
Stephen Massey (8)	179
Fintan Monaghan (9)	179
James Doone (9)	180
Ryan Reilly (8)	180
Sean Doone (9)	181
Emmanuel Watson (9)	181
Gareth Booth (9)	182
Adam Martin (8)	182
Gareth May (9)	183
James Haughey (8)	183
Peárse McKenna (9)	184
Eamonn Stitt (9)	184
Seamus Rooney (9)	185
James Keenan (9)	185
Patrick Fitzpatrick (10)	186
Kevin Carey (10)	186
Connor Laverty (11)	187

St Mary's Star of the Sea School

Anthony Gallagher (10)	188
Clare Aylward (11)	188
Leanne Finlay (9)	188
Kiefer Crandles (9)	189
Tammy-Lea Menagh (9)	189
Shauneen Quinn (9)	189
Maria McAnallen (8)	190
Rose Kennedy (8)	190
Michael Kane (11)	191
Mark McCrystal (8)	191
Áine Thorpe (9)	192
Stephanie Bonnar (9)	192
Christopher Taplin (10)	193
Caoimhe Cleary (8)	193

Iarlaith Rooney (8)	194
Christina Morrison (9)	194
Shirley-Ann Quinn (11)	195
Martin McCartney (9)	195
Stacey Hughes (9)	196
Kerry Fegan (10) & Jemma McIlveen (9)	196
Lorna Hughes (9)	197
Terri Rainey (9)	197
Lauren Ferguson (8)	198
Sorcha Convery (8)	198
Aine Mulvenna (9)	199
Maeve McIlroy (9)	199
Stephen Mullan (9)	200
Danielle McCormack (9)	200
Jamie McLaughlin (8)	201
Conor McLarnon (10)	201
Adeva McGuinness (10)	202
Shauna McCavana (8)	202
Sarah McCullough (10)	203
Bronagh McMahon (11)	203
Eamonn Privilege (10)	204
Shannon Davidson (9)	204
Christina Toman (11)	205
Carey Mullan (8)	205
Aoife Brown (10)	206
Shauna O'Reilly (9)	206
Colleen McGrogan (11)	207
Michael McMahon (10)	207
Leo Fegan (8)	208
Fearghal Conn (9)	208
Shannen Savage (9)	209

St Michael's Primary School

Katie Vinelott (8)	209
Emma O'Hara (8)	210
Claire Le Velly (8)	210
Julie McElroy (8)	211
Joseph Shields (8)	212

Ronan Smyth (8)	212
Catriona Acheson (8)	213
Catherine Rocks (8)	213
Claire McPeake (8)	214
Paula McKay (8)	215
Peter Brennan (7)	215
Clodagh Coyle (8)	216
Emma Martin (8)	216
Stephen Loughran (8)	217
Rachel Speak (8)	217
Christine Gargan (7)	218
Ruairí Cumiskey (7)	218
Fergus O'Brien (7)	218
Gregory Woods (8)	219

St Peter's Primary School

Michael Madden (11)	219
Emmanuel Barkley (11)	220
Megan Doyle (10)	220
Gemma Boyle (11)	220
Patrick Brennan (11)	221
Ryan McCormick (11)	221
Stacey Hodgkinson (11)	222
Brianne Reynolds (11)	222
Stacey Barkley (11)	223
Gemma McNerney (10)	223
Megan Ward (10)	224

The Poems

SUNNY DAY

The sun shines and lights up the mines,
All the sparkling bits of silver tin.
Please don't throw it in the bin,
The sun starts to bubble and burst,
Please don't die of thirst.
On the beach the children play,
But not with clay,
The water is crystal clear
And it's so very near,
But the haunted horse won't appear,
Suddenly! He appears but he chops off my head
And he calls for Father Ted.
By at the gallop he goes,
By at the gallop and then,
By he goes, back at the gallop again.
So the tide rises,
The tide falls.

Aidan Stewart (9)
Beechfield JMI & N School

SNOWY DAYS

The snow is here
And it is freezing
And I am warm in my bed
As warm as a blanket
Outside the snow falls
Softly, silently, ghostly.

Hayley Hawkes (9)
Beechfield JMI & N School

RAINY DAYS

Rain is cold and wet, splish and splash
Rainy days are coming today
Rain go away, you'd better say goodbye
And you'd better go away
Hayley and Dean thought it was going to rain
And so it did rain
Rain go away, you can stop if you want to stop
We stamp in puddles
Rain, rain, go away!

Samantha McClure (9)
Beechfield JMI & N School

THE SNOWY DAY

It is snowy today
As white as a page
I'm nearly in a rage
Too much excitement
With my friends
My name is Benj, I'm frozen to death
Icicles are nice
Water dripping like ice
It's nearly like a dream
I really do agree
This snowy day is so dreamy
And ice creamy to brighten up my day.

Nicola Stewart (8)
Beechfield JMI & N School

SNOWY DAY

Every snowy day
The whole world is full of snow
We all think we are dreaming
But we are not dreaming
It is for real
And everyone goes mad
Snowdrops are so white
You would think they are paper
The snow is freezing
I am like a statue
We always play snow fights
Everyone gets hurt
They get it wiped all over their faces.

Naomi Whyte (8)
Beechfield JMI & N School

A RECIPE FOR WINTER

Take some rain that has turned into ice
And dark, dull skies with a little bit of cloud,
Blend in hailstones with snow.
Add wind and leaves and maybe some bare trees,
Whisk some holly and a robin or two.
Mix sleeping flowers and snowflakes,
Garnish with frost and a bitter day,
Hibernating animals too
And simmering fir trees to finish it off.
Put in the oven
And that's your recipe for winter.

Rebecca Wilson (9)
Beechfield JMI & N School

Snow

The snow is a white, water substance
Which is about in wintertime
Kids have snowball fights
But strict people say it's a crime

The snow is tasteless and melts in your mouth
It is also soft, crunchy and cold
When there is enough snow to have a fight
Kids don't do as they're told

The snow is shapeless
It is scentless too
Watch out!
There's a snowball coming at you

The snow is melting
The leaves and flowers are starting to grow
I can't wait till next winter
I'm sure we'll say, 'Remember the snow a year ago?'

Bhargavi Chandrasekar (11)
Botanic Primary School

Snow

Snow is cold, snow is fresh
But sometimes it freezes my flesh
When the snow turns to sleet
It starts to soak my feet
Snow is white and very bright
Especially when the moon shines down at night
Snow is great when I play out at night
When I have a snowball fight.

Neil McAllister (11)
Botanic Primary School

SNOW

Snow is small and calm
Like a baby lamb
Snow is cold and wet
It turns to ice when it's set

Snow falls like a thousand small feet
Onto the ground, so clean and neat
Snow can fall quite silently
Lands on you and lands on me

Snow melts on your tongue
It's exciting when you're young
Snow, it feels so light
And it can't win in a fight

Snow tastes like an ice pop
And you can't buy it in a shop
Snow only comes about once a year
But it's lots of fun when it's here

Snow is so free
It blows around the Atlantic sea
Snow can be 1, 2, 3 inches deep
It grows deeper as we sleep

Snow can be strong and wild
And sometimes snow can be mild
Snow can be used for a snowman
Try to make him big if you can.

Emma Mitchell (11)
Botanic Primary School

DANCING DRAGON

I saw a dangerous, dancing dragon
It had tiny teeth
Its colours were ruby-red and glittery-green
It was a huge, hungry dragon dancing
It was fast and fierce
It liked to be humorous and tease
It's an ancient Chinese dragon
We all caught his cabbage
People were wearing silk saris
Some teachers had to try and make the dragon dance
Then it was really quiet
So we went back to our classroom in silence.

Michelle Veighey (10)
Botanic Primary School

THE CHINESE DRAGON

Humorous dragon
Dangerous dragon
Yellow and gold
Clever and bold

Fire-breathing dragon
Just lying down
It's going to lay
For the rest of the day

Crashing roar
On the floor
Lying on its knees
The Chinese dragon . . .

Andrew Hanratty-Mullan (9)
Botanic Primary School

THE CHINESE DRAGON

The Chinese dragon, the Chinese dragon
Was glittery gold and green
The Chinese dragon, the Chinese dragon
Was fast, fiery and fierce
The Chinese dragon, the Chinese dragon
Was loud, long and laughing
The Chinese dragon, the Chinese dragon
Was dancing, dangerous and deafening
The Chinese dragon, the Chinese dragon.

Aifric Smyth (10)
Botanic Primary School

THE CHINESE DRAGON

The dragon danced,
Danced on the dance floor.
Glistening gold, shining silver,
Ruby-red and white,
With big, bold, green eyes.
Chinese dragon, massive dragon,
Chinese dragon, huge dragon,
Chinese dragon, loud dragon,
Chinese dragon, quiet dragon,
Chinese dragon, sleeping dragon.

Fiona Butler (9)
Botanic Primary School

DANGEROUS DRAGON

The dragon is demonic, daunting and dangerous,
It has fast, fierce fire,
Its eyes are gold, gorgeous and green,
Its skin is like rock with red scales,
Bold, brave and tough,
Whenever it stamps an earthquake starts,
The city is a peaceful city,
But when the dragon comes . . .

Ciaran Bowen (9)
Botanic Primary School

DELICATE DRAGON

D ragon shiny, dragon scary
A ll are watching its hypnotic eyes
I n boisterous, bulging green, they capture your eyes
N ew, shiny sequins patterned round its body
T o its beat your heart pounds
Y ou, yourself caught in a daze from the beat of its stamping feet!

D ancing dragons are not fierce
R aging, reckless dragons running around our hall
A nd dangerous, dancing, dainty dragons make you wonder why
G one to scare some small people with its bulging eyes
O n and on it went, waking teachers from their sleep
N ever have I seen such a strange thing as a dangerous,
    dainty, dancing dragon dancing round and round!

Molly Davey (10)
Botanic Primary School

THE DRAGON DANCE

Dancing dragon, what a beast,
Stamping to the music.
Loud drums and cymbals sound in the background,
The dragon dancing to the beat.
Its head sways from left to right,
Its green eyes bulge and stare.
Gold, red and yellow
Wave all over the dragon.
Its ears flap and its eyelids wink,
Its mouth gaps at the crowd,
Looking for a feast.
A cabbage on the floor
Quickly gets picked up.
The dragon quickly scoffs it up
And shreds it to the crowd.
The children applaud the dragon long,
They cheer the dragon on.
Then suddenly, the music stops!
The dragon lies so still,
Everything seems to halt.
The dragon lies down for a sleep,
Until the next New Year.

Daniel Kerr (10)
Botanic Primary School

CHOCOLATE

Chocolate, chocolate, you are so nice,
Hot or cold, I do not care,
As long as I get it twice,
I have a sister and she says it's rare,
Though she eats it like a bear.

Jason Magill (11)
Carryduff Primary School

FOOTBALL

My team is Chelsea
They are in the Premier League
They play as a team
And never give up a fight

My team is Chelsea
They play with a lot of style
Our enemies are Spurs and Arsenal
Because they play in London too

My team is Chelsea
They play at Stamford Bridge
They play in blue and white
They're the best team in the land.

Benjamin McNeely (11)
Carryduff Primary School

THE STORM

Lightning and thunder thrash about,
The wind screaming past, rustles the leaves on the trees,
Hail comes hurtling down,
Rain batters the ground,
Dirt goes flying,
The sky is lit up by a flash of lightning,
Travelling at breakneck speed to the Earth,
Thunder rumbles,
Glass shatters,
Trees sway,
Birds seek refuge,
Nobody wants to go outside, it's just not safe.

Matthew Gibson (11)
Carryduff Primary School

MY FAMILY LIKES . . .

My little sister likes ice cream,
That is what it seems!
My little sister likes ice cream,
That is what it means!

My older brothers like music,
That is what it seems!
My older brothers like music,
That is what it means!

My older sister likes singing,
That is what it seems!
My older sister likes singing,
That is what it means!

My mum and dad like cooking,
That is what it seems!
My mum and dad like cooking,
That is what it means!

I, myself like playing,
That is what it seems!
I, myself like playing,
That is what it means!

Simon Brown (11)
Carryduff Primary School

PUPPIES

They're silky soft and lots of fun,
They love to lie down in the sun.
Their faces are cute and small
And they love to chase a ball.
Their coats are smooth or fluffy
And their tiny paws spread mud on the new carpet.
The puppy's bark is only a little yap,
They're perfect for cuddling on your lap.
It's now time for the puppy's first walk,
So get the lead, oh do hurry up!
When you come home after an enjoyable walk
The puppy flops in its bed,
Hear the soft breathing, the puppy's asleep.
I love puppies!

Kerry Gilmore (11)
Carryduff Primary School

HARRY

I have a cat called Harry,
Who likes to sleep and play,
When he plays he's as happy as Larry,
When he sleeps he does not make a peep.

My kitten likes the sun,
He thinks it's really fun,
He really hates the rain,
It's such a pain.

My cat does not like any other cats,
He has no time for them,
They must think he's a brat,
But he's my little gem.

Ben McGirr (11)
Carryduff Primary School

WESTLIFE

Westlife, Westlife, Westlife,
Oh how I'd love to meet you,
How I'd love to greet you,
How I'd love to keep you.

Shane, Shane, Shane,
How I love you so,
But I think you already know.

Bryan, Bryan, Bryan,
I adore you too,
But without you,
What would I do?

Nicky, Nicky, Nicky,
I don't like you as much as
Bryan, Shane and Gerard Mageean,
I'm sorry but that's just how I feel.

Kian, Kian, Kian,
You are a pain!
You are so not like Shane!

Mark, Mark, Mark,
You make me barf!
Why did you dye your hair?
You look so rare!

Westlife, Westlife, Westlife,
Oh how I'd love to meet you,
How I'd love to greet you,
How I'd love to keep you.

Danielle Clifton (11)
Carryduff Primary School

THE SEASONS

Winter is here
The children jump, shout and cheer
The snow is here

Spring is here
Snow has cleared
Time to jump, shout and cheer

Summer is here
School is out
Holidays are near, people jump, shout and cheer

Autumn is here
The crispy leaves are here.

Danielle Neill (11)
Carryduff Primary School

THE WEATHER

I hate rain,
It's a pain,
You don't get to go out to play.

I love sun,
It's way more fun,
Because you get to play all day.

I like fog,
It smells like a frog,
It's very misty too.

I adore snow,
You don't know,
Be careful or it'll get you!

Rebekah McClean (10)
Carryduff Primary School

BROTHERS!

Brothers are a pain in the neck,
but no one believes me, so what the heck.

They punch and push,
decide to throw you in a bush.

I really hate my little bro,
'cause when I start to hit and throw,
I get a whack around the head
and get told to go straight to bed.

Having brothers drives you insane,
having brothers, there's nothing to gain.

We don't like each other,
but I couldn't live without my brother.

Hannah McCaughan (11)
Carryduff Primary School

THE EAGLE

On top of the cliff
The eagle stands,
Looking at the rivers below.
Then quicker than a blink of an eye,
It was gone.
Soaring down to the river,
Trying to catch its prey.
Plunging into the water,
Fish in its grip.
Swoops back to its cliff,
To devour the fish in peace.

Tommy Burns (11)
Glenwood Primary School

THE BREAD'S JOURNEY

Lying on a plate,
Waiting to be eaten.
A hand is coming closer and closer,
It has lifted me up,
Its hands are so cold and wet.

It has put me in some place dark and damp,
The floor is beginning to move up,
Then I feel a sharp, hard thing touching me.
It has cut me up in lots of pieces
And I am falling down a thin hole.

Now I'm in a funny-shaped thing,
It is pouring something on me.
I feel like water coming down the tap.

Now I'm in a long thin tube,
I am going round fast,
I fall into another tube,
There I stay for a long time.

I am falling down,
It smells dreadful,
There are dead things in the water,
I wish I'd stayed on the plate.

Christopher Hill (11)
Glenwood Primary School

FLOWERS

Flowers are very pretty
They bloom in summertime
When you smell them
They bring you a smile

There's pink, purple and
Even blue, give them
To your mum
Say they're from you

Flowers grow in
Summertime, all through
Even in the garden
Or in Belfast Zoo.

Melissa Johnston (11)
Glenwood Primary School

THE OLD BOOTS

The old boots lay alone
In the old attic
No one wore them anymore
They were alone to rot
The nails at the bottom held them together
And steady, for someone to put them on
But they are now too torn
Their only dream is to be worn again
But it is much too late now
The man who wore them years ago
Has been dead for a long, long time.

Curtis Mawhinney (11)
Glenwood Primary School

Snow Clouds

When the stars come out at night
They chop up all the clouds
As the snow falls down to Earth
Separated from their friends
Nations watch for hours and hours
As it covers up the ground
More and more will fall
Then when it has stopped
It looks like a great white blanket
Then it starts up again
Only more gentle this time
And when it stops once more
Children go out to play
Then the big yellow sun comes out
And melts it all away.

Jason Beasant (11)
Glenwood Primary School

The Snow

The snow is crunchy
Watch it fall
The cars swish through the slush
My feet are soaking wet
You feel good inside
You are lovely and warm
Snow is like soft stones falling
They whizz past us
Then it all melts
And we wait till it comes again.

Nikki Smith (11)
Glenwood Primary School

THE MYSTERIOUS SHELL

It's not really a shell,
It's just a cover,
As the little fairies live,
They're called diminutive fairies,
The smallest of their kind,
No bigger than a tiny speckle,
They go all over the world,
They see the world,
But once a hermit crab sees the shell,
He snaps at the opportunity
To seize the shell for his home,
Once inside, the fairies can't escape,
The crab has a feast on these fairies,
So the next time you see a shell
That a crab has been in,
Don't think it's empty,
There's fairies living inside.

Dean Murphy (11)
Glenwood Primary School

SEA DRAGON

Swimming through the sea
Glistening, glossy white
Diamonds on the belly
The creature of the deep
It's been around for millions of years
Living on seaweed
Amongst the rocks.

David Crane (11)
Glenwood Primary School

THE ICING FROM THE SKY

The icing from the sky
Is so white and pale
That it tastes freezing cold.
Children play in our icing,
Making balls and huge men too.
They have a carrot nose and button eyes
And a white body that melts in the sun.
Until the fluffy clouds
Turn grey and heavy once again.
The cloud people from the sky always
Sprinkle the icing onto our streets and roads,
Turning them into crunchy cakes
For us to have some fun in winter,
But when it happens,
We have to wrap up warm,
Because it's cold and makes us shiver.

Samantha Seaton (10)
Glenwood Primary School

THE SNAKE

The slimy snake
Slithers in the grass
Hunting for its prey

Along comes a mouse
And the snake is lurking behind the grass
Waiting for its moment

A couple of minutes go by
Then his chance comes
Wraps around the mouse
And says, 'Here's my breakfast.'

David Hussain (11)
Glenwood Primary School

TUBBY

A tubby cat with long thin whiskers
Lies in the jungle grass
And waits for a little black mouse
He shoots out his shiny claws
His teeth are reddish-white
With the bloodstain of his prey
He pokes his tail up in the air
With excitement and the little black mouse comes
Slash, the mouse is dead
The tubby cat drags the mouse away
To its back garden to eat
In the sunshine.

Brooke Goodwill (10)
Glenwood Primary School

OLD BOOTS

I am very old and aged
My laces are gone
No one wants me anymore
All I do is rot away
Wondering what the world is like
But no one wants to wear me
So I'll never explore
I'm left here with only hope
That someone will wear me
I can only think of what the world is like
But never really know.

Ryan Azzabi (11)
Glenwood Primary School

WATER

There's nothing healthier than water,
Not a thing,
People drink it hot or cold,
People drink it young or old.
There are different kinds of water,
Tap, river, rock and Evian.
Water is transparent and very shiny,
It tastes plain.
Some people like fizzy water,
But I like it normal.
You can get water in a bath,
In rain or snow,
Water even makes you grow.

Ellen Hill (11)
Glenwood Primary School

THE SNOW

Crunch, crunch, crunch goes the snow
As it is walked on,
Slush, as the cars drive by.
Snowballs being thrown
At each other,
The roads, dark and grey,
People freezing cold.
Mountains covered with snow,
Like a pale white blanket.

Lisa McCaw (11)
Glenwood Primary School

HORRENDOUS BOOTS

Then he soaked them by mistake,
So put them out to dry.
The sky started to rumble, crash and thunder,
Lightning started, it was frightening,
Then the boots were zapped,
Then they turned ragged.
The carpenter then was surprised,
So he tried the boots on,
He started thinking evil thoughts,
He then did something horrible.
No one saw him do this thing,
He stabbed a man with knives,
Then he took the boots off wondering,
What have I done?
That night when everything was dark,
He burnt those gruesome boots,
Never to be brought back again.

Jason Barrow (10)
Glenwood Primary School

FALLING SNOW

You see snow fall, gently hitting the ground
You say, 'It looks like flowers coming from the sky.'
You walk outdoors to see it lying beside you,
When lifting it, you will feel the roughness of the snow.
The cars will go along the road and make a slushing sound
And soon the snow will melt away.

Claire Wilson (10)
Glenwood Primary School

THE SHELL GHOST

The shell was really odd,
It looked different.
We were scared,
We walked away,
All except one,
He walked towards it,
Getting closer, closer, closer.
He lifted it,
The wind was blowing,
We were frightened.
Suddenly a ghost came out,
We screamed and ran away.
It started to chase us,
It grabbed me,
I started to cry,
It looked like something Picasso painted.

Nicholas Wilson (10)
Glenwood Primary School

FOOTBALL

Up and down it goes
Whizzing around like a bullet in the sky
Whizz, whizz, whizz . . .
It goes with a *thump!*
When it hits the player on the head
Thump, thump, thump . . .
Bang when it hits the player's foot
Like dynamite exploding
Bang, bang, bang.

Marcus Kane (11)
Glenwood Primary School

THE DRAGON

Crash! Bang! Pitter-patter! Pitter-patter!
The storm raged on
The pirates and their captain have been shipwrecked you see
So the captain ponders if shelter will be
'Ah, a cave!' he shouts. 'We'll go in there. Will we?'
They struggled up the windy hill,
Heads held high
And then they hear a voice from deep inside.
'Humans,' the wretched voice snarls, 'you will not come in,
For I have treasure beyond your wildest dreams
And I know that foolish man will steal it ruthlessly.'

Now a chap called Peter, or Crossbone to his mates,
Gets scared so he runs away sharpish –
Clever Peter, or Crossbone to his mates.
The captain urges his men inside,
'You don't want to be a coward like old Crossbone,' he says.
And the pirates so easily led,
Follow him inside the cave
And unfortunately came to a very sticky end –
They were consumed by the dragon, legs first!
For there were no jewels, only a very smart dragon –
So the moral of this tale is;
'When threatened by a dragon
Run -
Or you may lose your head!'

Louise McLaughlin (9)
Holy Rosary Primary School

DEATH

Death is black
Smells like bare, cold bodies
Tastes like mouldy bread
Sounds like diseased voices locked behind chambered doors
Feels like ripped-out hearts
Lives in a deep, dark forest -
Death.

Sarah Montgomery (9)
Holy Rosary Primary School

LOVE IS . . .

Love tastes like sweet, red apples
Smells like beautiful pink roses
And looks like a lovely summer's day
Love sounds like a baby bird hatching
Feels like a little puppy curled up in its basket
Love is sweet.

Laura Curry (9)
Holy Rosary Primary School

SADNESS

Sadness is as clear as a tear
Tastes like sour milk
Smells like flowers dying in a beautiful field
Looks like a pond that was once filled with wildlife
But now is completely empty
Sounds like cries of pain in a dark, cold cellar
Feels like losing your heart that was once red, now black.

Bebhinn Schaible (9)
Holy Rosary Primary School

ALIENS HAVE ALWAYS PUZZLED ME

Aliens have always puzzled me.
When I looked through my telescope
What did I see?
A saucer flying over my friend's house,
As quickly and quietly as a mouse.

An alien knocked on my door,
I kicked him (must have been sore!)
He fell hard on his head upon the floor,
I even tore apart the clothes that he wore.

Ever since, they've left me alone,
I told my friend the story in an undertone.
I didn't want anyone else to hear,
I think aliens have a new fear!

Ciaran Fitzpatrick (10)
Holy Rosary Primary School

VIKINGS

When there is a storm
The Vikings cannot sail 'til morn
But when they do sail
Their boat is as tough as nails
And when they land
They can stand
Against the fighting men
That that country sends
After they plunder and loot
Home on transport
Other than foot.

Conall Bailie (10)
Holy Rosary Primary School

MY PET KANGAROO

My pet kangaroo
Is nothing
Like me and you.
He hops all day,
He hops all night,
Has big, big ears
And long, long legs.
So he will jump out
And give you a fright.
Skippy is his name -
He is very bright.
If you argue,
He'll beat you in a fight.
He has brown fur and yes,
A long tail -
So don't ask,
He's not for sale.

Aaron Black (10)
Holy Rosary Primary School

IF I HAD A PET DRAGON

If I had a pet dragon
I would make him roast the turkey
Instead of having every year
Disgusting beef jerky

If I had a pet dragon
I would make him fly me to the North Pole
And back
In the time it takes to pile a haystack.

Paul Stelges (10)
Holy Rosary Primary School

THOUGHTS OF A FLOWER

Flowers, flowers everywhere,
Do they feel? Do they care?
Do they enjoy the summer breeze,
As it rushes through their leaves?

Do they ever dream to fly
Past the moon and stars and sky?
Do they long to sing and prance
As they watch the rushes dance?

Do they want to talk and natter
As they hear the children's chatter?
Do they ever wish to be
Just like you and just like me?

Aoife Rose O'Reilly (10)
Lough View Integrated Primary School

SNOW

I like making snowmen
I like the way they glow
I like my little sister
And I like playing in the snow

The snow is like a blanket
But very, very cold
The flakes are all different
Or so I've been told

My mum is in the garden
Having a snowball fight
She's not in my team
But that's *alright!*

Selina Lewis (10)
Lough View Integrated Primary School

DARK ROOM

When I go to bed at night
Shadows come to give me a fright.
Like rock climbers they climb up the wall,
They lose their grip and then they fall!

I turn on the flashlight and I think,
Wow! Where have all the shadows gone now?
On the wall using my fingers,
I make a dog and little stick figures.
I see a monster on the wall,
But it's my imagination all along.
I turn off my light and just like that,
Here comes a shadow big and fat,
I close my eyes, not a peep,
I lay myself down to sleep.

Amie Martin (11)
Lough View Integrated Primary School

SCHOOL

Through the gate and into jail,
A seven year sentence with no prevail.
Says the officer at the front,
'Dear girl, you are but very blunt.'
The bell rings loud and I am proud,
I've made it one more day,
But as for tomorrow,
It will bring much more sorrow,
But until then however,
I'm free.

Emma Osborne (11)
Lough View Integrated Primary School

MAGIC BOX
(Based on 'Magic Box' by Kit Wright)

I will put in the box,
A ten foot high honeycomb ice cream,
An everlasting wish machine
And the sweet smell of victory.

I will put in the box,
An expensive jewel from the Queen's crown,
The sound of a peanut butter sandwich roar
And the massive skull of a red T-rex.

I will put in the box,
All the glowing stars in the universe,
The fear of a giant tarantula crawling all over me
And a moon rock from the distant moon.

I will put in the box,
My never known long-lost grandad,
The booming sound of a volcano erupting
And the first toenails of a baby.

My box is fashioned from fire, wind and rain,
With baby's tears on the lid
And gold grass in the corners.
I shall hide my box in the darkest, deepest, coldest place on Earth,
So that only I can find it!

Maeve McQuillan (11)
Lough View Integrated Primary School

MONTHS AND SEASONS

March has my birthday
Summer has the sun
Christmas brings the presents when the year is done
But best of all is August
When football season's begun
When the ref blows the whistle
We will all have fun.

Conor Locke (10)
Lough View Integrated Primary School

CHRISTMAS IS...

The decorations round the tree
The Christmas treats for my family and me
Candles everywhere I go
The sound of children in the snow
The smell of turkey in the oven
The taste of the lovely stuffing
When the church bells start to peal
Then we know it's time for our meal
The lovely food that we all share
The smell of roasting food in the air
All the presents in my hands
Hearing carols from brass bands
Snowflakes falling from the sky
Take a slice of lovely mince pie
All the tinsel round the tree
The presents are just for me
The children's cheeks are roaring red
I think it's time to go to bed.

Jenny Clements (11)
Malvern Primary School

Rudolf

R eindeer
U nder stars
D ancing
O ver rooftops
L ightly
F lying.

Demi Sanlon (8)
Malvern Primary School

Shark

S ly hunter, is no good
H unting for sea food
A shark attacks when he smells blood
R ams into a dolphin with a thud
K ing of the sea, just leave him be.

Naomi Wilson (8)
Malvern Primary School

Shark

S hark, sly, slithering slug
H ateful, hungry, horrid thug
A ttacks, so be afraid, be aware but do not dare
R ebuke or he will ram, so run to the rock if you can
K iller coming, kick, escape from the king
   for he is mean.

Ashleigh Gaynor (8)
Malvern Primary School

LIMERICKS

There once was a boy called Colin
Who truly lived in Holland
He fell in a hole
Now his face was like coal
And wished he now lived in Poland

There once was a girl called Jenny
She once found a bright, shiny penny
She thought she was rich
So she acted like a witch
But now she doesn't have any!

Billy Boomer (10)
Malvern Primary School

SHARK

S   hark slithered and slunk
     with a smile most unpleasant
H   orrible monster, watery peasant
A   ttacking, cunning, he ain't messing
R   un, run as fast as you can
     don't be caught by the shark, man
K   ing of the sea, I taste bitter
     please don't eat me.

Alan Montgomery (8)
Malvern Primary School

FOOD ALPHABET

A is for apple, so juicy and sweet,
B is for buns we all like to eat.
C is for chocolate, brown or white,
D is for doughnut, delicious and light.
E is for eggs, round and small,
F is for fish, which I don't like at all.
G is for grapes, small but sweet,
H is for hamburger, my ideal treat.
I is for ice pops, I like ice cream instead,
J is for jam, you can put it on bread.
K is for KitKat, a chocolate bar,
L is for lemon, tangy and sour.
M is for Monster Munch, spicy and munchy,
N is for Nutella, crispy and crunchy.
O is for oranges, juicy and sweet,
P is for pears, I don't like to eat.
Q is for Quality Street, a box of chocs,
R is for ribs, as hard as rocks.
S is for salt, we put on our chips,
T is for tomatoes, watch for the pips!
U is for ugly fruit, which I've never seen,
V is for vinegar, disgusting with beans.
W is for watermelon, green and red,
X is for Xmas stuffing, I love it with bread.
Y is for yoghurt, different flavours you can buy,
Z is for Zinger Burger, it's hot and dry.

Elizabeth Mawhinney (10)
Malvern Primary School

My Teacher

M y teacher is very creative.
R eally, really kind.
S he is reliable.

M y teacher is magic.
C heers us up when we are sad.
N ever seen without a smile.
E xcellent teacher.
I s kind of crazy.
C hosen to be our teacher and I'm glad.
E xcitement is what she gives us.

Philip Morrison (8)
Malvern Primary School

Shark

S wim, swim as fast as you can
   that shark is going to get that man.
H ow do I know? How do I tell
   That a shark has a good sense of smell?
A girl will kick you on your gills
   now she knows how to kill.
R un, run, run away
   there's another shark in my way.
K eep on moving, don't look back
   if you don't want to be a shark snack.

Shannon Brownlee (8)
Malvern Primary School

SHARK

S harky jaws around the sea
   is he eyeing me for his tea?
H e slithered and slunk
   with his fin like a punk.
A shark will attack when he smells blood
   taking aim, then *thud, thud, thud.*
R un, run, run if you see a shark
   'cause they will eat you, light or dark.
'K ing of the sea, I am,' he would sing
   that sly, evil, fearless thing.

Natasha Johnston (9)
Malvern Primary School

SHARK

S harks are sly, sharks are slick
   come on out and play hide-and-seek
H ammerhead is very scary
   but they eat fish, so do not worry
A great white shark is gliding this way
   I wish I hadn't come swimming today
R un, run as fast as you can
   this shark has been known to eat a man
K iller shark is around me, *help*
   I'd rather this shark liked sea kelp.

Rebecca Verner (8)
Malvern Primary School

LIMERICKS

There was a young man called Scream
Who played for a spooky football team
He scored many goals
Then did forward rolls
And now works with ice cream

There was a young girl called Juliette
Who drove a fancy Corvette
Down the street she dashed
And then she crashed
Now she looks like a lumpy courgette.

Colin Johnston (11)
Malvern Primary School

SHARK

S harks are fast and frightening
   they move through the water like lightning
H ungry sharks are very cunning
   if one comes near, you'd better start running
A shark is coming this way
   I wish I didn't come swimming today
R un to dry land, don't look back
   that shark thinks you'd make a tasty snack
K ing of the sea, please don't eat me
   I would make a bitter tea.

Karl Harper (9)
Malvern Primary School

A GOOD TEACHER

A good teacher should always help you at work
and be kind to you when you are stuck.
They should not shout too much!
It is important to treat pupils the same.

A good teacher cares for you when you get hurt
and they need to like children.
If we have a row or are cheeky to our teacher,
they must forgive us.
Last but not least, a good teacher
should give you fun work.

Christina Keenan (9)
Mersey Street Primary School

DAYDREAMING

Miss Carson thinks I'm doing my work
but I'm daydreaming about going outside

Miss Carson thinks I'm learning my spellings
but I'm daydreaming about becoming rich

Miss Carson thinks I'm listening
but I'm daydreaming about growing up

Miss Carson thinks I'm reading
but I'm daydreaming about getting a job.

Christopher Leebody (10)
Mersey Street Primary School

DAYDREAMING

Miss Carson thinks I'm doing my work,
But I'm daydreaming about becoming rich!

Miss Carson thinks I'm reading,
But I am dreaming about going on holiday.

Miss Carson thinks I am marking books,
But I am dreaming about getting a job.

Miss Carson thinks I am doing my work on the computer,
But I am dreaming about winning the lottery.

Miss Carson thinks I am going on an errand for her,
But I'm thinking about swimming at the Olympics.

Megan Todd (9)
Mersey Street Primary School

BULLYING

B is for bad, this word describes bullies.
U is for understanding teachers who help the victims.
L is for them laughing at you as they torture you!
L is for laughing at you when the bully hurts you.
Y is for yelling out loud when the bullies beat you up.
I is for feeling ill when you have to go to school to face the bullies again!
N is for the nervous feeling when they come towards you!
G is for the greatness they must feel by doing this to others!

Chelsea Charlesworth (10)
Mersey Street Primary School

FAMINE

F is for the famine that started in 1845.
A fter the famine stopped, all the potatoes started to grow again.
M any people died because of the famine.
I n Ireland the potato blight started in 1845.
N early everybody went to the workhouse, it was terrible!
E migration was very popular, most went to America for a new life.

Jade Morrow (11)
Mersey Street Primary School

A SPOOK IN THE NIGHT

In the castle if you look,
There will be a scary spook.
Scaring people in the night
And making a shiver run down your spine.
This king of creeps comes when you sleep
And he'll capture your soul forever.
He'll take you along,
In his hand quite strong,
To his castle away in the woods.
When you're there,
You'll get a scare
And he won't treat you good.
He'll make you his worker
And give you yucky food
And you're not allowed to break the rule,
Never, never, never.

Niamh McCusker (8)
Our Lady of Lourdes Primary School

HOLIDAYS

Holidays are fun
Lying in the sun
Swimming in the pool
To keep me nice and cool

Eating lots of chips
And watching all the ships
Drinking lots of Coke
With my friends and folk

Playing in the sand
Working with my hands
I think I see a jellyfish
It is time to scram.

Ciara Lynch (9)
Our Lady of Lourdes Primary School

LIFE AS A LIZARD
(As a pet)

Stuck sleeping within this glass tank
I wonder if I should give any thanks?
Eating crickets all day long
Wondering where I even came from
Taken away from the golden beaches
Where I could relax and enjoy ripe peaches

What did they want with a tiny old lizard?
My head is in a complete blizzard
Don't get me wrong, in here I'm protected
Given food to keep me strong
Never neglected, no strife
What's wrong with my life?

Georgia Behan-Doyle (9)
Our Lady of Lourdes Primary School

MY WISH

I wish I had a little pet
A cat, or maybe a dog
Every evening after tea
I would take it for a jog

I would like to call him Mr Max
And teach him lots of tricks
Like standing on a beach ball
And fetching me some sticks

I would like a dog and not a cat
Cats are not much fun
A dog would always play with me
And a cat would sleep in the sun.

Gareth McCrellis (8)
Our Lady of Lourdes Primary School

FANTASY LAND

My fantasy land starts like this,
It has rides and games with funny names.

My water park has slides with funnels,
That go into dark, dark tunnels.

It has scramblers and a dirt track,
I have a mansion with a yard full of sweets out the back.

I would have a Coca-Cola ocean
And I would swim in it like a magic potion.

I wish that this was all real,
'Cause that would be a nice end to this wonderful tale.

Christopher Gormley (8)
Our Lady of Lourdes Primary School

PIRATES AND PARROTS

My name is Captain Grey Beard,
I'm a pirate, greatly feared,
On my ship are forty men,
I write my story with a pen
And now to get the treasure.

I sailed from the town O'Mally,
On my ship, the Golden Galley,
We sailed the seas a thousand day,
Through stormy winds and come what may,
I found Skull Island at last!

Skull Island is a spooky place,
The massive cave is like a face,
There are dead bodies here and there,
They will give you quite a scare,
They searched for treasure just like me!

Me and my men were at the cave,
We were waiting there bold and brave,
Then we heard a roaring noise,
'Get your cutlass ready boys,'
Then we saw a giant!

He swung his club round and round,
He squashed my men to the ground,
Heads and arms and legs they fly
And once I thought I saw an eye,
'I'll have to kill this monster!'

My parrot flew in causing trouble
And had the giant seeing double,
I stabbed the giant in the chest,
Took the jewellery and the rest
And that's the truth, me-hearties!

Nathan Kelly (9)
Our Lady of Lourdes Primary School

MY NEPHEW

My little nephew is just six months old,
He loves to laugh and play with a toy,
When he lies on the floor, over he rolls,
He's a clever chap and a cute little boy.

His name is Eoín and I love him a lot,
He has two front teeth and bright blue eyes,
When it's time to go to bed, Eoín shouts and bawls and cries.

He loves me to sing and dance for him
And he tries his best to join in,
He jumps up and down on his mummy's knee,
Moving his arms and leaping for glee.
My nephew's one of the best things that's happened to me.

When he gets big, I'll take him out,
We'll play with my friends and I'll look after him well,
He'll enjoy our games without a doubt.
He can cheat to win and I won't tell,
He's the most adorable little boy that ever was born,
His hair is the colour of a field of corn.

Whether he laughs or cries, it makes no difference to me,
Because the key to my heart he holds for free.

Megan McCarthy (8)
Our Lady of Lourdes Primary School

My Dog, Rags

My dog, Rags, he eats so much
His tummy sags

He goes
Flip, flop
Wig, wag
Zigzag

I love Rags and Rags loves me
He goes
Flip, flop
Wig, wag
Zigzag

Rags is the best dog ever
He goes
Flip, flop
Wig, wag
Zigzag.

Woof! Woof!

Eimear Rosato (8)
Our Lady of Lourdes Primary School

My Sister

I've got a sister, her name is Eimear,
Some people say she looks like me.
She is always copying and following me,
She's like my Mini-Me.
She is annoying and fun
But she is the one
And after all, she's my Mini-Me
And I love her.

Naomh Rimes (8)
Our Lady of Lourdes Primary School

MY BEST FRIEND

I have a best friend,
Her name is Naomh Rimes,
She is always very helpful,
She is always very kind.
She helps me when I'm stuck,
She helps me all the time.

When I feel down,
She is always around.
She always is there,
About in thin air.
I'm never down if she is around,
'Cause that is a good friend.

I like my best friend, Naomh,
I like her very much.
I think about her day and night,
I really hope that we don't fight.
So that was my best friend,
She is the best, better than all the rest.

Megan Reid (9)
Our Lady of Lourdes Primary School

My Mum!

My mum is the best,
She always lets me phone friends
And lets me go everywhere,
She is the best mum in the world!

Mum is special,
She likes to keep me safe,
My mum has that warm smile
That keeps me company every day.

My mum is sweet and kind
And gentle as can be,
I can smell her scent of lavender coming towards me,
I don't know how to say this,
But I think she is so much cooler than me!

Toyah Warnock (8)
Our Lady of Lourdes Primary School

Manchester United

Man U I support
They're a very good team
Probably the best
They are even supreme

With Beckham and Giggs
Forlan and Scholes
Lots of them score
Fabulous goals

Yesterday The Hammers they beat
By six goals to nil!
The West Ham supporters
They must have been thrilled!

Sean Loughran (9)
Our Lady of Lourdes Primary School

MY FAVOURITE DAY

On my favourite day, no Weetabix for me,
It would be Coco Pops and chocolate for breakfast, lunch and tea.

I would play my PS1 from morning until night,
With no mum or dad to shout at me or sister to make me fight.

I would swing into my tree house with my blankets in the air,
Pretending to be a pirate, fighting with a bear.

I would read my books and Beano and plan some nasty tricks
And ask my friends to help me to collect lots of sticks.

We would build a secret stick hut to keep out all the girls
And if the girls came near us, we would cut off all their curls.

We would sleep in a tent in the garden, all through the night
And hope there would be visitors, 'cause we'll give them a fright.

Kilian Gargan (9)
Our Lady of Lourdes Primary School

FIZZ

I've got a secret, a little one,
Well no, it's not real,
It's actually quite a big one.
Come closer and I'll tell you.

I've got a friend, she's my best friend,
My only friend,
I play with her and care for her,
I share my thoughts and my smiles and tears.

You do know you can't tell anyone
Because they'll just laugh and think I'm daft
Because *Fizz* is invisible.

Grace Prenter (9)
Our Lady of Lourdes Primary School

THE SEASIDE

At the seaside there are lots of shells
And the sounds of the sea's waves
Sound like bells

If the children spy a rainbowfish
They are allowed to make a wish
It might be for silver, it might be for gold
It might just be that it doesn't turn cold!

Here is the sun, here is the sea
Hear the children shouting with glee!
Here is my bucket, here is my spade
Look at the sandcastle that I just . . . *made!*

Look at the crab in my hand
Follow my footprints in the sand
Now that I am in my bed
I think of the seaside, in my head.

Claudia McCracken (9)
Our Lady of Lourdes Primary School

A MISERABLE DAY

It's a rainy old day
And I don't get out to play.
I want to play some games,
Such as making funny names.

I want to go up to my room and make up plans
And not get stuck in traffic jams,
Maybe I should build a hut and invite my friends to play,
Then maybe it will not be such a miserable day!

Matthew Deighan (8)
Our Lady of Lourdes Primary School

ANIMALS

Animals, animals running free,
Animals, animals running with glee.
Fish swimming in the sea,
Birds nesting in the tree.

Pigs, pigs they love to snort,
Dogs, dogs they love their sport.
Sometimes tall, sometimes short
Or big and ugly like a wart.

The animals went in two by two,
Helped by Noah and his crew.
Up they went into the floating zoo,
Led by a monkey called Sue.

Declan Coghlan (9)
Our Lady of Lourdes Primary School

MY FEARS

My fear of heights makes me scared,
I just wouldn't stand and glare,
I'd rush away downstairs.

I'm afraid of Mum screaming when there's a mouse,
Until it's caught, she moans and groans about the house.

I don't like going out too late,
It makes me shiver like jelly on the plate.

I also wouldn't like an earthquake,
For large holes it does make.

Don't forget about nettle stings,
They bring me out in lumpy things.

Dermot Trainor (9)
Our Lady of Lourdes Primary School

MY DOLPHIN

The glimmering sea where the dolphin lives,
Is as still as still can be,
Then suddenly a fin appears,
As he leaps across the sea.
A sparkle of magic, the shape of an arch,
Makes me feel so happy to be,
Wishing I could swim with my dolphin,
To his world in the deep, deep sea.
The squeak of his voice
And the smile on his face,
Would make me follow his lead,
To that underworld place.
It might be cold and probably dark,
With even a chance of a passing shark,
But I know that I'd be safe,
Because I'll always trust his friendly face.

Conor Marley (8)
Our Lady of Lourdes Primary School

MY PET LIZARD

The lizard has a very long tail
And four short legs
But it can run faster than a snail

Some lizards are green
Some, like the chameleon
Can change their colour
So they can't be seen

They eat crickets and snails
An other lizards' tails
They eat worms and slugs
And other disgusting bugs

But I still think lizards are cute
And I'd like one as a pet
But my dad says no
Maybe someday that's what I'll get!

Sophie Magee (9)
Our Lady of Lourdes Primary School

THE SEASIDE

At the seaside I play all day at the rocks
And at the docks

There is a sea
With beautiful dolphins that are staring at me

There is a sun as bright as can be
Which is always shining on me

There are fish deep down in the sea
Who always wriggle at me

There is seaweed in the sea
That always jiggles at me

The wild waves always white
Make the sea look blue and bright

Then the rain comes and spoils our fun
But I know next time I'll have more fun.

Rory Millar (8)
Our Lady of Lourdes Primary School

HOLIDAYS

'Where shall we go on holiday this year?' said Dad.
'How about Turkey I hear it's not half bad.'

'What about Spain?'
Oh no!
Not that again.
The sun was hot, the pool was cold,
The food was horrid and the apartment was old.

We liked France, the children agreed,
For remember the park and the pond with the ducks to feed
And peddling down for baguettes, chocolat et pain
And the crepes avec sucre made by the funny man.

'Wait,' said Mum, 'I've got a plan,
Let's all go to the Isle of Man.'

'You've got to be joking!' Dad said with a fright,
'But I suppose at least it would be a short flight.'

'Ah! Portugal!' said Aimee, 'That's my favourite scene,
I'd love to go back to the zoo marine.'

'Well, sorry kids but this year
The budget is low,
So down to Cushendall we'll just have to go.'

Larragh Mann (9)
Our Lady of Lourdes Primary School

SNOW

Snow, snow has far to go
It falls high from the sky
To us down below

It changes our world to a beautiful white
And in the early morning
Is a wonderful sight

It changes my mood
Makes me feel excited and good
Snowball fights, sliding and sleighs
As friends we play, never forgetting this day

Cold feet and rosy cheeks
To our homes we go
Seeking some heat

But soon from our windows
The snow beckons again
Off we go, dreading the rain

It could spoil all the fun
Wash the snow all away
We want to hold on
For just one more day.

Rachel Bannon (9)
Our Lady of Lourdes Primary School

EMMET

I know sometimes he is a pain
But he's really rather sweet
When he is being good
He cuddles up and plays with my feet

He loves the *bath*
So don't say it too loud
Because he always makes a mess
When he splashes all around

He's got red, curly hair
Like a cute little angel
But when he empties the toy box
Mum says he's a devil

He's really quite loveable
And bad a little bit
He's terrific and terrible
My baby brother, Emmet.

Clare Burns (8)
Our Lady of Lourdes Primary School

OLD JACK FROST

It's wintertime
It's getting cold
And old Jack Frost
Is getting bold

He sprinkles windows with ice
And there is snow on the ground
And old Jack Frost
Is nowhere to be found

With him he brings the
Promise of spring
When the leaves come out
And the birds all sing

But it's not spring yet
So keep warm if you can
There will be more cold weather
Says the sneaky old man!

Claire Doyle (8)
Our Lady of Lourdes Primary School

I Want To Be A Footballer

I want to be a footballer
And play upon a pitch,
But when I come home,
It looks like I've been in a ditch.

Henry's my superstar,
He gets one thousand pound an hour,
But now I'm only an excited youth,
Ain't that the awful truth.

So I'll have to wait a little while,
To get a chance at that big trail,
I have to be good and not be rude,
To get my dream to be on the team.

Conor McLarnon (9)
Our Lady of Lourdes Primary School

No One Needs To Know!

My secrets are for me to know and me to know only,
If someone finds out about one of my secrets,
Then I would beg them to keep it that way,
Because the world is not like that,
The news travels faster than you think.
There it goes, from one person to another,
Just like it's news to people but it is personal to me.
When someone finally tells it to me,
I just nod along pretending I am listening and saying I haven't
                    heard it before.
I finally ask who it's about
And they go, 'Don't you know? Doesn't it sound familiar to you?'
And now I know, it's not a secret any more.

Jessica Barrett (11)
Rosetta Primary School

WHY?

This old woman in a home,
Getting fed her lunch,
Disabled, blind and weak,
Nor can she now speak,
Starts to wonder why,
Why it had to be her?
For once she led a happy life,
Happy, plain and simple,
Realised that life wasn't all good,
As she soon found out,
Her house, her husband and all her fortunes,
Were all burnt away,
For the people who had done this,
Still have not been found,
She'll never know,
Know, who did this,
Just sits and thinks
To herself,
Why? Why did this happen to me?

Amanda Herron (11)
Rosetta Primary School

MY SCHOOL TRIP

My class and I on a bus,
On our way to sea,
On a trip, we tell some jokes,
Oh how lovely to be me,
Laughter fills the bus with glory,
Oh happy to be me,
Me and my friends sing together,
As happy as could be.

Amy Harrison (10)
Rosetta Primary School

MY BEST FRIEND

My friend was always there for me
Like when I fell off my bike
He helped me up when I got hurt
And I did the same for him
There was a day we played around
And bounced the ball on the ground
Then the day came to an end
So I said goodbye to my best friend

The next day
I hoped he was there to play
But he wasn't there, not to be seen
I couldn't believe my eyes
As I saw the *For Sale* sign
I didn't get a chance
When the day came to an end
To say goodbye to my best friend.

David Moutray (12)
Rosetta Primary School

THE WEATHER IS BAD TODAY

The weather is bad today,
I wish I could go out and play.
The sky is all bare,
The birds are not there.
I wish I could go out and play.

Laura Gibson (11)
Rosetta Primary School

THE GRANDFATHER CLOCK

Oh it stands there,
Oh so still,
Ticking and chiming all day long.

When you are quiet,
You can hear it tick,
Tick-tock tick, then *bong*,
Oh you don't have to be quiet to hear it.

You hear it at night,
You hear it during the day,
You can hear it upstairs,
You can hear it downstairs,
You can hear it in your head.

Oh the grandfather clock,
Tick-tock tick.

Kirsten Dodsworth (11)
Rosetta Primary School

THE GRANDMOTHER I NEVER KNEW

The grandmother I never knew,
I never knew her name,
I never knew
If she was fat or thin, small or tall
I never knew
If she'd like me.

But there are two things I know,
She was my mother's mum
And I have another one.

Adam Campbell (11)
Rosetta Primary School

MY PET RABBIT

I had a pet rabbit when I was about six,
It had big ears and hair black and white.
We let it have a play just for some fun,
But . . . a black-haired, green-eyed stalker was on the loose.
As it leapt into the air, I ran to save my pet,
But when I got there, the cat had already dashed away,
Heedless of the carnage he'd left.
As my bunny stood very still, red drops of blood dripped,
Tears slowly and gently ran down my face.
The stalker had taken his life
And a little bit of mine.

Matthew Weir (10)
Rosetta Primary School

FREDDY'S FLYING FIESTA

Here it comes,
Here it comes,
Flying down the street,
Freddy's flying fiesta.

Turning to the left,
Turning to the right,
Swerving all over the street,
He hits the brakes,
But it is too late,
Freddy's already at the bottom of the street.

Stephen Craig (10)
Rosetta Primary School

FAMILY

Holly, Mia, Ewan,
Granny, Granda too,
The things the closest to my heart
Are the people around me who care,
Emma, John, Katie,
Paula, Simon, Keith,
Some live far,
Some live near,
Some across the road,
The farthest away in London.
But when we're all together,
At Christmas or in the summer,
We act as if they're just around the corner,
But when they go and it's quiet,
We just pick up the phone.

Susan Burrell (10)
Rosetta Primary School

THE FORGOTTEN BABY

A baby is for life, not just for show
When he cries, he goes unheard
So sits alone, afraid and scared
From the fears of the world
And his tears surround him
In the crowded town
He doesn't make a sound
But inside his heart cries
You can see the pain in his eyes
He is forgotten, alone, a wandering soul.

Rebecca Shaw (11)
Rosetta Primary School

PARADISE

Crystal clear waters
Golden sandy beaches
Palm trees swaying in the breeze
As I lie beside the pool
With the beaming rays of the sun in my eyes
I realise I'm in paradise
But not for long
As I leave for home in the morning
I say my last goodbyes
And see again, the grey skies
Of home.

Alannah Scott (11)
Rosetta Primary School

A MAGICAL PLACE ON EARTH

The water glistening in the golden sun
The sun reflecting off the water
Gently, softly, happily, the glittery, twinkling water sways,
Rising upon the golden beach,
The steamy, hot, iridescent sand,
This magical place on Earth,
Where you can see the perfect beach,
With the most exotic twilight in the distance,
So quiet, so calm, so amazing,
The Caribbean beach.

Shannon Ferguson (10)
Rosetta Primary School

MY CAT

My cat is a girl and her name's Lucky!
She loves to hide in a box or behind a tree
She will always be hard to see
She likes to hunt her prey, fast or slow
They'll never know what bit them
She rolls in the house anywhere she likes
On the floor or on the chair, she never annoys us
Because she's my lovely cat
But one sad day
We saw in the bush
She was dead
Knowing those starry eyes
Looking at me, not knowing what to do
A tear came out of my eye and then another
Why? Why? Why?

Alan Foster (11)
Rosetta Primary School

LOVE

Love is all you need
To know your heart is free
As I sit in the rain
And I think of love again
I know my heart is free

As I see that boy go by
A tear fills my eye
My heart fills with pain
So I think of love again
My heart then becomes free.

Catherine Magill (10)
Rosetta Primary School

Two Goldfish

Two goldfish, two goldfish,
Was my only wish,
Two goldfish, two goldfish,
In a shop of fish,
Five pounds each,
Ten in total,
Oh, I really wanted them.

One day my mum got me them,
Happy, joyful, delighted I was,
Two goldfish, two goldfish,
In a tank of mine,
Gave them food,
Lots of food,
Looked after them well.

One day, one sad day,
Before I went to school,
One goldfish, only one,
Was floating on the water,
Tears came to my eyes,
Water dripping down my face,
Oh, how sad I was then.

One week later,
One more died,
I felt like there was nothing left,
Nothing left in the world,
Nothing left but me.

Claire McCaul (11)
Rosetta Primary School

CAT AWARENESS!

I go to bed and dread the worst that can happen,
In comes the cat, the biting highness,
The queen of the fangs awaits her meal.

She now jumps up onto the bed
And climbs under the quilt,
I'm sweating like mad,
My face has gone sad, then she stops . . .

She waits a minute,
Then she goes for my feet,
I am now in pain,
She goes for my feet and my legs,
Then I throw her through the air,
Ascending then descending,
In a ball of spiteful fury.

I am now crying, my bed is all wet,
Her highness jumps up as I jump down
And run upon the stairs,
Down I go,
But my mum says I was dreaming,
But it must be true . . . right!

Christina Elliott (11)
Rosetta Primary School

JAMIE LEE

There was a young girl called Jamie Lee
She was as small as a hairy bee
Her eyes were green
She was very mean
And she lived in an apple tree.

Hannah Barnes (8)
St Bernadette's Primary School

FISH

Slippery
Slimy
Feels like jelly
Swims through
The ocean like
A thunder ball
Fast, speedy
Never stops until you
Feed it
If you eat it, it runs through your belly
Like a lump of jelly.

Una Beales (9)
St Bernadette's Primary School

MONKEY

Clever,
Cheeky,
Friendly,
Monkey,
Swinging tree to tree,
Quickly,
Carefully,
Funnier than a clown,
If you ever disappear, monkey
I will come and get you,
Monkey,
Cheeky monkey.

Emma Bonner (9)
St Bernadette's Primary School

THE BOA CONSTRICTOR

I am a boa constrictor,
I am caged behind a transparent square,
I used to slither through the long grass of the rainforest,
Hiss at my terrified prey and strangle those squeaky birds
As I filled them with poison.

But now I am stuck behind a glass window
At the Belfast Zoo.

Joanne Savage (11)
St Bernadette's Primary School

A YOUNG GIRL IN SALOU

There was a young girl called Sue
And she went to Salou
She had a fright
In the middle of the night
By a ghost that said *boo!*

Lorraine Loughran (8)
St Bernadette's Primary School

BUTTERFLY HAIKU

In the summer air
Butterflies flap their bright wings
Like a gentle breeze.

Nicole Bradley (10)
St Bernadette's Primary School

CATS, CATS, CATS EVERYWHERE

Fluffy cats,
Big cats,
Everywhere you go cats,
Wild cats,
Pet cats,
Diving off the wall cats,
Fast cats,
Slow cats,
Everywhere I see cats,
I don't like cats,
Go away!

Carla Butler (9)
St Bernadette's Primary School

THE MOON

The moon
    Twinkles
Like a big star in the sky
    Sparkles
Like a golden ring just brand new
    Glistens
Like a polished pebble cleaned always
    Gleams
Like a creamy pearl on a black dress
    Lights up
Like a sparkly, shiny, yellow sun
    Shimmers
Like a silvery pond in a deep dark forest.

Joleen Clarke (11)
St Bernadette's Primary School

THE MOON

The moon
   Shines
Like a golden round ball
   Sparkles
Like a diamond ring
   Twinkles
Like a star far away
   Gleams
Like a cream pearl on a black dress
   Shimmers
Like a silvery pond in a garden.

Alison Curley (11)
St Bernadette's Primary School

THE MOON

The moon
   Shimmers
Like a white diamond lying in a black box
   Sways
Like a white dress on the washing line at night
   Rests
Like an eye going to sleep on a white pillow
   Glistening
Like a pan when it's washed and put in the cupboard
   Flies
Like a plane through the midnight sky
   Shoots
Like a bullet high in the pitch-black night.

Nikita McMullan (11)
St Bernadette's Primary School

THE MOON

The moon
 Glistens
like a firework in the night sky

 Glitters
like a golden ring on a black, velvet cushion

 Shimmers
like a shooting star on a black dress

 Reflects
like a river flowing through the dark forest

 Lights up
like a street light in the starless street

 Twinkles
like a rocket in outer space.

Fiona Hall (11)
St Bernadette's Primary School

DOG KENNING

Cat chaser
Bone eater
Lip licker
Car chaser
Paper carrier
Food snatcher
Garden digger
Cat hater.

Roisin Carey & Caitlin Corbett (11)
St Bernadette's Primary School

Snow

Out of the grey heavens flow,
The crisp white fluffy snow,
Slowly, silently, swirling,
Carried by the icy wind twirling,
Engrossing the Earth out of sight,
In a cold woolly blanket of white.

The enticing blankets of white
Say it's time for a snowball fight,
We better have fun,
Before it's done
And swallowed up by
That great big evil sun.

Jack McCambridge (10)
St Bride's Primary School

Inis Oirr

The sand is yellow
The sea is clear
The sky is blue
In *Inis Oirr*
The roads are rocky
The fields are small
But in the pub, it is best of all
To me, I love the beach
And sand
And I love to wash my feet
And hands.

Emily Kate Herbert (10)
St Bride's Primary School

SNOW

Snow fell silently through the night
Under the cover of darkness
And on waking, everything
Looked white, fresh and clean
Trees, which the day before were bare
Wore their cloaks of white with pride
Houses looked like they had new roofs of cotton wool
And cars, as if they were covered in meringue
Children rushed to play in the white delight
Adults groaned at the thought of dangerous journeys
And all concerned wrapped up in scarves, gloves and hats
Next day, the white had turned
To dirty, melting brown
The joys, delights and games in the snow
Now just precious memories.

Adam Valente (10)
St Bride's Primary School

THE DRAGON

Fiery dragon flying so high
Up above in the cloudy sky
Down looks the mighty beast
Preparing his next tasty feast
He swoops down and kills his prey
He'll be back another day
Flying back to his lair
Without pity, without a care.

Jéri Cronin (11)
St Bride's Primary School

AT THE ZOO

Be careful what you
Say and do
When you visit
At the zoo

Don't laugh too much
At the chimpanzee
He thinks he's as
Wise as you or me

Don't giggle much
Around the giraffes
They get upset
When you laugh

Don't stare too long
At the seals
They only like people
With their meals!

At the birds
Be careful too
Especially when
They drop their poo!

Don't make fun
Of the camel's hump
He's very proud
Of his great big bump

Treat them as well
As they do you
And you'll always
Be welcome at the zoo!

Katie McMullan (10)
St Bride's Primary School

I Need Some Inspiration

I don't know what to do,
My head's in such a tizzy.
I have to write a poem tonight
But I'm really much too busy.

'No more than thirty lines,' she said,
That seems a lot to me.
I'd rather play some tennis or
Sit and watch TV.

It's really hard to concentrate,
There's so much going on.
My brain is so exhausted,
I think I'm going to yawn.

I need some inspiration,
Something from the heart.
I wish I were better at English,
I wish that I were smart.

Today's my brother's birthday,
We're having a special tea.
Turkey and ratatouille,
I bet you wish you were me!

My mum is calling me for dinner,
My granny is here with the cake.
My poem is still not written,
I give up - for goodness sake!

Nicola Quinn (10)
St Bride's Primary School

JACK FROST

He's nipping at the window
And painting everything white.
He's a gleaming white ghost
That comes in the night.

He dances around the garden,
When everyone's asleep.
While through the windows
His grinning face does peep.

He covers every corner,
Nowhere does he miss.
Then joins the North Wind for a party,
'Ah,' they cry, 'this is just bliss.'

When everyone awakens,
He tiptoes quietly away.
Then the children wrap up warmly,
So they can go out and play.

He's nipping at the window
And painting everything white.
He's a gleaming white ghost
That comes in the night.

Eavan Prenter (10)
St Bride's Primary School

My Little Sister

My sister has curly hair
And it is really fair
She plays Barbies during the day
And always wants her own way

She washes the window by herself
And pulls everything off the shelf
She likes to look in the mirror
But she just laughs at herself

She used to lie in cows' hay
And now tries to make up her own play
She loves her baby-minder
And there's nobody who is kinder

Her birthday is in April, early in the spring
When the new lambs are born
And the birds start to
Sing.

Marie Louise Farag (10)
St Bride's Primary School

Computers

Computers, computers driving me insane,
The password is denied again and again,
These computers have a box full of brains,
On computers you can play lots of games,
I get so annoyed by it, I want to destroy it,
It drives me mad, it stretches my brain,
It drives me up the wall until I fall,
Computers are everywhere, every day,
I wish these computers would just go away.

Ronan McDaid (11)
St Bride's Primary School

WORLD CUP FEVER!

The countdown is on,
Excitement is mounting,
I just can't wait,
Two weeks and counting.

Thirty-two teams,
From all over the world,
A riot of colours,
As the flags are unfurled.

Every country hoping,
To bring home the glory,
Every player waiting,
To tell his own story.

The last minutes of the match,
The stadium is still,
The referee blows the whistle,
The final score, one-nil!

Oliver Tumelty (10)
St Bride's Primary School

WINTER

W inter is a cold time of year,
I like to have snowballs fights, the snow I do not fear,
N obody can catch me, I am as quick as a fox,
T owards the snow, here I come,
E veryone is afraid, their feet are getting numb,
R eferee shouts, 'Away from the fight.' I was so sad that night.

Katie Connolly (10)
St Bride's Primary School

THE BELFAST BEAST

The Belfast beast
Is up for a feast
This, thought the beast
Is true
But where, oh where to go?

A stroll through Stranmillis?
A swill from Cave Hill?
Some meat from High Street?

Or maybe, just maybe
A crawl to City Hall
Might tempt those vicious jaws?

But alas in the sky
Shines something quite high
The sun has brought the light

As it ran, the beast thought,
Until the next night . . .

Michael McAuley (10)
St Bride's Primary School

SNOW

Snow, snow
O fluffy snow
I hate to see it when you go
It steals our precious snow away
When you are up there
I really think it isn't fair.

Claire Whittley (10)
St Bride's Primary School

MY FAMILY

To tell you the truth
My family's pretty strange,
There are monks, there are French
And there are Danes.
Well, we'll just start with my uncle Jim,
He's been outside the solar system,
He said it wasn't exciting at first,
Until he saw a planet burst!

Now, let's get down to the real junk,
My grandpa Teddy, he's a monk.
He says now he wants to retire,
(I think his boss just wants to fire!)

He's not so enthusiastic there,
You just have to bow in prayer.
He always says he was a gymnast,
Until he saw the giant pin mast,
He said he was on the Olympic team,
Until he ate a bucket of ice cream!

It's now time for my grandma Kadd,
You won't believe this,
But she's completely mad!
Once when I was at her house,
She tried to dissect a ginormous mouse,
This may be something you ought to teach,
But she tried to do it with a barrel of bleach.
So there you go,
It's all done,
It's very impressive all in one,
Oh, don't worry, there's lots more,
This is just the apple core!

Helen Quinn (10)
St Bride's Primary School

MY MUM'S TEN COMMANDMENTS

My mum has ten commandments, that she puts on a list
And she makes me - I'm telling you, she really does insist,
That I should be obliged to obey
The rules, she says, day after day -
The rules on that blasted sheet,
On which the writing's done so nice and neat.
'Would you like to see the commandments?' she says to me
                                                    and my brother,
'Well, here they are for you, one after another:

1. Be in bed before half-past eight
2. Always say 'Thank you' and 'That's great'
3. Give me a hand whenever I ask
4. Always complete your boring tasks
5. Be polite to every guest
6. Always try and do your best
7. When in Mass, be deep in prayer
8. And I must choose the things you wear
9. Don't put your shoes on my seat
10. Keep your bedroom nice and neat

I know it doesn't sound much fun,
But after all, I am your mum!'

But unfortunately for my mum
I don't obey a single one!

Elspeth Vischer (10)
St Bride's Primary School

ANIMALS

Horses galloping up and down
Makes me happy, I never frown
Riding them is such fun
Striding across the fields in the sun

Cats love playing with yarn
And of course sleeping in the barn
Scrabbling about playing cat and mouse
Wrecking all the chairs in the house

Playful puppies run around
Trying to grab the ball from the ground
Falling asleep on my lap
A day of torture, the poor little chap

He's big and cuddly, he's a polar bear
With his huge eyes and lovely white fur
He lives in the Arctic with all the snow and ice
I'd love to live there, an igloo would be nice

Horses, cats, dogs and bears
There are plenty, most in pairs
There are lots of every type
All are counted, right down to the pike.

Rebecca Campbell (10)
St Bride's Primary School

SNOW

Snow, oh snow is falling
Oh, how much I hate being inside
Stuck in a classroom doing nothing
But looking at snow

How cold it is when it is snowing
And slippery it is too
Can't even go on my bike

But you can have a snowball fight
And that is great fun
You can also build a snowman in your garden
Or go down hills on a sleigh

Snow, oh snow is falling
Oh snow, why is it snowing?

Ciara McFerran (10)
St Bride's Primary School

I MISS GRANDPA

I miss my grandpa very much
I miss his warm and gentle touch
I miss the way he'd look at me
His eyes as deep blue as the sea
I miss the smile he always had
Even when I was naughty and bad
I miss the way he used to speak
Even when his throat was weak
I miss the wrinkles on his head
I really miss him now he is dead.

Rebecca Copeland (11)
St Bride's Primary School

MY DRAGON

I have a dragon,
One of a kind,
He's different to all other dragons,
He's hard to find.
He lives in a cave
And comes out at night
And lights up the area
With his wonderful light.
He has claws as sharp as nails
And a tail that swishes and swipes,
A thunderous roar,
A blazing fire,
He's a scary dragon,
But he's *mine!*

Bronagh Macartney (11)
St Bride's Primary School

FRIENDS

Saturday morning, I got up from bed
'It is your birthday,' my mummy said
Excitedly I devoured my breakfast
And thought the time would never pass!

One by one, my friends arrived
And at last all were there by five!
Together we went to 'Lord of the Rings'
And were frightened at all the murderings!

Back at the house we played and played
Until our Domino's was made!
Sweets, chocolate and birthday cake
But time was up, for goodness sake!

Connor McMurray (10)
St Bride's Primary School

DESERTED

I have been deserted for as long as I can remember,
I think it's been since last November;

I lost my parents in a shipwreck
And now I don't have a speck;

I have some mangoes from the trees
And lots of honey from the bees;

I play with the animals to keep myself content,
But I'm bored with the sloths to the extent;

I search the island for my parents,
I think something is keeping me from them,
Almost like a metal fence,
I yearn to get out of this pen
And see my parents alive again.

Christian Boyle (10)
St Bride's Primary School

TREES

Trees' roots like sprawling spiders,
Tree trunks like bars of steel,
Autumn leaves like sheets of gold,
Falling down like shot planes.
Forests like floods of green,
Glowing green like a radioactive spill.

Trees are shiny like silver birch
Or dark brown like a spruce fir.
Trees can be rough like the chestnut
Or nice and smooth like a eucalyptus tree.

Denis McKaigue (11)
St Bride's Primary School

MY CAT, DIZZY

My cat, Dizzy
She's fat and she's lazy,
She sleeps on the ground
And won't follow you around.

My cat, Dizzy
She's fat and she's lazy,
She's white with some black
And likes a wee snack.

My cat, Dizzy
Is so awfully lazy!
She just will not play!
(But sits yawning all day!)

My cat, Dizzy
Is not always so lazy!
When you leave out her dish,
She'll run to the fish!

Zara O'Reilly (10)
St Bride's Primary School

SPRING

The larks singing their sweet melody
And the breeze blowing,
The lush grass to and fro,
The grasshoppers chirruping
And the frogs croaking.
The heather and the broom up on the moor
And the spring lambs are gambolling happily.

Charlotte Doran (10)
St Bride's Primary School

THE WITCH IN DISGUISE!

The witch in disguise really does despise
All children tall and small,
Fat and thin,
Her nose like a pin,
She'll drive you up the walls!
She yaps and snaps,
She rants and raves,
With an evil taste,
For making children cry,
She always casts an evil glance in the corridor,
As *I* go by!

I know she's really a witch,
Because she told her shrew,
But!
Hush up about my secret
Or she'll be after you!

Rachael McKinney (10)
St Bride's Primary School

COLOURS

Colours range from black to blue,
Straight lines,
Bendy lines
And polka dots too.
To leave the world without colour
Is something I could not do.
Chimney tops, sofas too,
Everything has colour, do you?
We all love colours
And I hope you do too!

Sarah Niblock (11)
St Bride's Primary School

THE BLACK DRAGON

The black dragon beats his mighty wings
The black dragon, most powerful of things

The black dragon's scary orange eyes
Flashing through the dark night skies

The black dragon's skin, as black as ink
The scariest sign, the people think

The black dragon's tail swishes violently
The black dragon breathes fire powerfully

The black dragon's horns are ram-like
The black dragon's claws are eagle-like

The black dragon sits in his dark cave lair
The black dragon thinks himself proud but not fair.

Lorcan Gallagher (11)
St Bride's Primary School

HOMEWORK

Homework, homework, I hate it all!
Maths, geography and science
It drives me up the wall!

Teachers say it's good for you
I don't think they are right
How about you?

We have to work till 3 o'clock each day
Why do more work when we go home?
I say!

Daniel McCrea (11)
St Bride's Primary School

HUNTING DRAGONS

There it is,
Over here,
Under there,
It's trapped in a cage.
Slice it,
Spear it,
Kill it,
Wrap it and send it to Japan.
Before we knew it, it broke free
And then it counted one, two, three,
It blew and burnt a coconut tree.
Faster than the speed of light,
It took out a sword and began to fight.
Oh no, we were going to fail,
But to our luck it started to hail.
The dragon cooled down and could not fight,
So we sliced it up, nice and right,
No more killing mice in the Smith's kitchen.
Oops!

Aoife Leonard (11)
St Bride's Primary School

FRIENDS

F un and laughter all the time,
R arely a day that isn't fine,
I 'm so lucky to have them,
E very one's a total gem.
N ever lonely, never sad,
D on't worry, even when times are bad,
S uch good friends I've always had!

Niamh O'Hare (11)
St Bride's Primary School

FIRE-BREATHING DRAGON!

I spied a dragon one autumn night,
But then I heard a large voice say,
'Has my dinner come to stay?'
'No,' I said, and simply sighed!
I ran, at least I tried . . .

Then at last he followed me
And he nearly ate me up,
I ran and ran as fast as I could
And then a puff of smoke came out.

What could I do, I just stood!

I stared at him with trembling jaws,
But then you can't escape my powers.
He gobbled me in one big bite,
Oh, that was such a terrible night.

Orla Campbell (11)
St Bride's Primary School

THE BEACH

The beach, the beach, the great beach
With sand so soft
The waves push the little rocks off
Where kids bury their dads
And others just jump in the sand
The mums just watch and see
As their little ones play in the sea
High in the sky, the hot sun shines
On seagulls flying high
As I leave in the hot summer day
I hope to return to the beach one day.

Laurence Magowan (11)
St Bride's Primary School

THE BULLY

There is a place
Where learning is fun
Fun for some
But not for one

This is because I am
Being tortured by another
His name is Big Bob
His best friend, his brother

They always have
Their hair in spikes
And ride around
On stolen bikes

Every day when the
Lunch bell calls
He is always hanging
Around the walls

He waits until I'm all alone
Making my weary way home
Then he would threaten
There may be no weapon

Now I know
The old saying is wrong
Sticks and stones
May break my bones
But names will still hurt me

This has gone over the top
I am going to tell -
Full stop!

Una Grace (11)
St Bride's Primary School

FLOWERS

Flowers, bright beautiful flowers,
Rich in colour all summer long,
Dying out in winter's storm

Flowers, bright beautiful flowers,
Shooting up in springtime
And growing on and on

Flowers, bright beautiful flowers,
Tulips, poppies of every colour,
Dancing in the sun.

Flowers, bright beautiful flowers,
Rich in colour all summer long,
Dying out in winter's storm.

Maria Martin (11)
St Bride's Primary School

SNOW

Snow, snow, snow
Falling to the ground,
Making not a single sound,
It lies there all crisp and fresh,
White as white can be.

Snow, snow, snow,
Falls around wintertime.
I love the snow, I'm sure so do you,
I love having snowball fights
And making snowmen too.

I wish it would snow . . .

Anastasia McBride (11)
St Bride's Primary School

My Favourite Things!

I like to swim in the pool,
I think it's really cool!
I fly up and down the lane,
But my efforts are sometimes in vain.

I like acting and putting on plays,
It helps to pass the rainy days.
I listen to loads of CDs,
The noise brings my mum to her knees!

I like playing tennis as well,
When my partner and I really gel.
With my little blue racquet,
When the ball comes, I really smack it.

Netball is fun every week,
Trying to get on a winning streak!
Passing towards the goal,
Heck, we're on a roll!

Oh well, dream on until next week!

Sarah McSparron (11)
St Bride's Primary School

White Rapids

We go to the white rapids every day
We go down to swim and play
We do this every day
When it is nice and bright
One day we went down and got a terrible fright -
The rapids had frozen over with ice.

James Trainor (11)
St Bride's Primary School

I HATE GETTING OUT OF BED

Under the blankets, it's very *cosy*
And I'm feeling nice and *rosy*.

Above the blankets, beyond the *bed*,
The light shines through and hurts my *head*.

But I know I have to get up and *out*,
Or else I just might get a *clout*.

And when I'm out and on the *floor*,
I'm so sleepy, I can't find the *door*.

I wish getting out was just a *dream*,
Because everything outside the bed is so *mean*.

Now that you've heard everything I've *said*,
You'll understand why I hate getting out of *bed!*

Caroline McElroy (11)
St Bride's Primary School

DRAGONS

A dragon has scales from 1 to 20
A dragon has toes that curl like bows
A dragon can fly from here to there
A dragon can fly just about anywhere
They're the source that doesn't care
I think dragons are lazy everywhere
To me they have red eyes that glow
And teeth that they're ashamed to show
They also breathe red-hot fire
That looks just like a lava shower
Now this is where the poem ends
Good luck with the dragons, my good friends.

Owen Farnan (11)
St Bride's Primary School

THE PEACE SEEKER

In the early morn,
By the banks of the river,
A dark figure walks,
Cloaked in blackness.

His name is not spoken,
For the ancient willow they hold a secret.
His footsteps are not heard no more,
For he is only a shadow of what once was.

His memories still lie in the murky bottom,
But he will never make the same mistake again.
For the water it still quivers with its memories of the scream,
When shadow paces his last steps.

In the darkness of night he haunts,
Haunts your dreams,
Haunts your very soul,
Draining the happiness from within you.

He is yearning for the happiness he lost,
The happiness which was stolen from him.
His soul cannot rest,
For he is the peace seeker.

Olivia Lucas (11)
St Bride's Primary School

THE VIKINGS

Those crazy savages from the north visited me one day,
They came in longboats so fine
And sailed right into the horseshoe bay,
They jumped ashore demanding plunder and wine.

What little resistance we had ran to meet them,
But we were slaughtered by those northern lads,
They ran to our monastery and stole our gold and gems,
They slaughtered the children, mums and all dads.

They broke down our doors with bloodstained swords,
There was death in their eyes,
They wanted booty for their lords,
They were a fearsome sight covered in dyes.

The survivors ran for nearby caves,
While the Vikings searched for more treasure,
We knew we would become slaves
And used to their cruel pleasure.

Kevin Shannon (11)
St Bride's Primary School

THE WINTER

W indy weather, wet and cold
I n the garden so full of snow
N ever want the snow to melt
T hrough the window I can see children playing happily
E vening brings the frost and ice
R acing and sliding down the slopes on our sledges with high hopes.

Conn McGrath (11)
St Bride's Primary School

THE SHETLAND PONY

Up on top of an old dusty hill
Lived a small Shetland pony
It was as black as night and all lumpy and bony

See it run, see it gallop, see it frisk all day and night
See it jump, see it roll in the ungreen field

But when you look upon its muddy face
You see it has no freedom
But as I look down to open the gate
It nudges me with its nose

As it canters down the hill, it whines lowingly
As I wave goodbye and give a sigh and walk off lonely.

Maeve McMullan (11)
St Bride's Primary School

WINTERTIME

W eary winter days are here to stay
    wonderful summer days are far, far away
I ce on the roads makes the cars collide
    and we all slither, slip and slide
N ippy winds take us by surprise
    and blow down things of all shape and size
T oboggans and sleighs race all around
    across the crisp, white snow all over the ground
E ndless days of cold, frosty weather
    and children play huddled together
R obins are the only ones left behind
    so they build warm nests in any tree they can find.

Caoimhe Sheppard (11)
St Bride's Primary School

MY FIRST FLIGHT

I sat on the cliff edge all day
Looking across at the bay
I hadn't the nerve to budge
I know I needed a nudge
I felt so lonely
Oh if only
I could spread my wings and join my dad as he sings
'Come fly with me'
Suddenly I saw a bee
But he didn't see me
Without thinking I made a leap
And plunged very deep
Spreading my wings full span
I flapped them up and down
Before I knew it, I had reached Ballygown
Hurray, I have made my first flight.

Catherine Macaulay (11)
St Bride's Primary School

SUMMER

Summer is here for every year,
Summer is here, I am here,
Summer is good because we're all here.

Summer is the best time of year,
Summer is hot but not too hot,
Summer, that means days outside,
Summer is long but not long enough.

Summer means long days outside,
Picnics for my friends and I,
All out together, summer, summer, I love summer.

Emma Beattie (11)
St Bride's Primary School

CHOCOLATE

Chocolate is my favourite treat,
I eat it every day,
I think it's lovely, yum, yum, yum,
It's nice in every way.

My dentist says it's bad for me,
But I don't really care,
If my brother stole some,
I would pull his hair.

My mum took it away from me,
She said, 'It's far too bad.'
But then I screamed and shouted,
I was very sad.

I love it very, very much,
It's better than the rest
And just in case you haven't guessed,
Chocolate is the very best!

Beth Gilmore (11)
St Bride's Primary School

MY WINTER POEM

The hills are white and covered with snow,
The roads are busy and the traffic is slow.

School is a pain because you can't get out
To run around and play and shout.

You can build a snowman big and round
And watch it melt to the ground.

Ross Whittley (11)
St Bride's Primary School

PRINCESS PERFECT

People say she is so perfect,
Brilliant, in every way,
But no one has seen this princess
Until this very day . . .

The castle claimed she was unique,
Intelligent and fair,
They said she had a special talent,
Which was extremely rare.

But someone in the village
Cried out with great alarm,
'Why have we not seen our princess
Who has both beauty and charm?'

The villagers marched up to the castle
And demanded to see this girl,
The king looked terrified and shocked,
In his robes and precious pearls.

Finally after hours of waiting,
Before each villager went back to their house,
Every single person saw the princess,
A pathetic little mouse!

Christine Gallen (11)
St Bride's Primary School

FOOTBALL FANTASY

F ancy Dan, that's who I am
O ut on the football field
'O lé!' the crowd shout as I dribble about
T he defenders confused by my skills
B ang, it's gone wide and I swallow my pride
A llowing myself to forget
L urching and searching, I pick up the ball
L eaving it square in the net.

Joe Begley (11)
St Bride's Primary School

TRANSPORT

There's lorries, cars, buses and trains
So much that they would drive you insane

There's more types than you could think
Painted all different colours, even pink

There's some which go on track
And there's others which travel on tarmac

There's cars which are good in speed
And others in which style is in need

There's some lorries which carry goods and gold
And ships likewise except in their hold

They run on tracks and it's called a train
Carries people like the plane.

Daniel Nolan (11)
St Bride's Primary School

Dolphins

A dolphin is a wonderful thing
It's very brilliantly smart
It can do so many funny tricks
But I don't think it's good at art

The bottlenose dolphin is most common
It's everybody's favourite one
It eats tasty fish all day long
And likes to play in the sun

Have you ever thought what it would be like
To be a dolphin so fine
You could swim in the ocean all day long
And never get bored of fish to dine

But some poor dolphins are stuck in a zoo
What could we do to help?
We need some support to get them out
And free them one and for all.

Jane Mulholland (11)
St Bride's Primary School

Fright

It was the stroke of midnight,
I got such a fright,
I saw something so bright.
A young woman sweeping down the stairs,
Upon her feet, nothing she wears,
Behind her, a man without a head,
Her husband who is also dead.
They sweep downstairs, this is where they go,
Where they come from, I do not know.

Stephanie Donald (10)
St Bride's Primary School

SOME PEOPLE

Some people are bad
and others are just sad.

Some people are good
and others are just plain rude.

Some are kind
and others are blind.

Some people are ill
and others just want to kill.

Some people are smart,
but some do not want to take part.

Some people are tall
and some are small.

Some people are black
and some people are white,
but that doesn't matter,
so we shouldn't fight.

In this world, this world,
this big, big world,
everyone's different.

Thomas Southern (11)
St Bride's Primary School

THE SEA

When it's early at the beach,
The water laps upon the sand,
Slowly moving to and fro, to and fro.

Now it's flowing faster,
Yet gently splashing
On the pebbly beach.

It's building up its strength,
Crashing and bounding
Against the tough rocks.

Calmer and calmer it grows
And soon like before,
It is slow and gentle once more.

Aoife Carberry (11)
St Bride's Primary School

MY TEACHER

My teacher is an alien
He comes from planet Mars
He gives us homework and makes us work hard
Even though he sits there and bosses us about
If only we were older
We could boss him about!
English, maths and science
Must be the only words he can say!
'It educates you,' he says (more like it bores us to death!)
If I had a wish I know what it would be -
I would wish to get my own back
And send him out to sea!

Rose McKeogh (10)
St Bride's Primary School

NATURE

Nature is made in different ways
We see it at night and we see it in the days

Every mountain is worth a penny of waste
And every fruit off a tree has a better taste

The roots of the trees and the green, green grass
Are much better than pollution, chemicals and gas

The world is not for wasting, it's for people to share their love
While others have to lie in their deathbeds and watch from
                                            the sky above

So I tell you now we should work as a team
To bring in the goodness and to fight off the mean

Nature is to be loving and nice
And we will find it somehow and make the world a *paradise!*

Jenny Putt (11)
St Bride's Primary School

SPRING

I like spring because
the weather gets warmer,
the days are long and
I get to play with my friends!

The birds like spring because
there is a lot of warmth and food,
they like the flowers
and the spring showers!

Alexandra Gilroy (10)
St Bride's Primary School

Chips

Chips, chips, glorious chips,
There's nothing quite like them for fattening your hips (who cares!)

I don't care, come what may,
I have chips on Saturday (every!)

Maris Pipers, Kerrs Pinks,
They're the best, don't you think? (I do!)

I think my mum deserves a crown
If she can make them crispy and brown (my favourite!)

Bread and butter with lots of salt
And don't forget the vinegar malt (to make butties!)

Why the chip shop do we pass
When going in is just first class? (I agree!)

Each day after school I ask my mum,
'Any chips today for my hungry tum?'
(Usually 'No' except for Saturday of course!)

Laura Boyle (11)
St Bride's Primary School

Snow Time

S now is falling thick and fast
N ow we hope that it will last
O n my sleigh, I speed down the hills
W e're off to the biggest hill in town

T o jump, slide, slip and run and have some fun
I n the powdered, speckled snow, something hit my head
M y dad had thrown a snowball at me, then we all went home
E verybody's sad because it's all gone away.

Peter McAuley (10)
St Bride's Primary School

BABY CHLOE

Mum and Dad have gone mad,
Baby Chloe has been very bad.
Chloe has wrecked Mum's dish
And even eaten my goldfish.
Last week she set the house on fire,
When I tell people, they say I'm a liar.
Chloe is only one
And look at all the things she's done.
On top of all that, she cries all night,
Oh, there she goes ripping up my kite.
Our neighbours called 999 because of no sleep,
My dad said she didn't make a peep.
The wind around here has a very high gale
And our neighbours are putting their house up for sale.

Clare Toner (10)
St Bride's Primary School

MY FAVOURITE DAY

Saturday is my favourite day
I get up late and play and play
We go to the pool in the car
I don't mind, it's not so far

Later on my friends will call
We go to the park to play football
After that I have my tea
And settle down to watch TV

Before too long it is late at night
I like to read with the light
When Mum comes in for one last look
I'm tucked up cosy with my book.

James Rooney (10)
St Bride's Primary School

I Say No!

The tree's branches spread across the sky
And we wonder will you ever die?
The tree says, 'No!'
So we say, 'Will you ever go?'
The tree replies, 'No!'

'We want you to go so we can see sunlight.'
'All you will see is a building site,' said the tree
'So I will never go, I can't, so I won't.'

The tree asked us, 'Why do you want me to go?'
We said, 'We don't really know.'
The tree asked, 'Is it because I take up too much space?'

As he looked down at the little boy's face,
The boy said, 'Can I go?'
The tree said, 'Yes.'

Máire Toner (10)
St Bride's Primary School

The McAdoos

Next door is like a zoo
It has every animal and some insects too!

There are cats, rats and kangaroos
And they all belong to the McAdoos!

They aren't like me and they aren't like you
They don't mind the smell of elephant poo!

They let the monkeys share their loo
But what do you expect from the McAdoos!

Aoife Corrigan (10)
St Bride's Primary School

THE OCEAN

Way down at the ocean floor
There's lots of things to see
There's animals down there
Nothing like you and me

The fish swim all day and night
The big, huge sharks
Give me such a
Fright

The ocean's packed with
Plants too
They quiver around with nothing to do

Oh, the ocean
What a sight
I dream about it
Every night.

Donal Keenan (10)
St Bride's Primary School

HALLOWE'EN

Hallowe'en, Hallowe'en, such a pretty sight,
Fireworks in the morning, afternoon and night,
Some people dressed up as ghosts and ghouls,
Other people dressed up as silly little fools,
Mummies, wizards, witches too,
Scare some people with a big *boo!*
Parties go on all night and day,
You could not stay away,
Now it's time to say goodbye,
Hallowe'en is over now.

Niamh Muldoon (10)
St Bride's Primary School

WINTRY WEATHER!

When winter comes,
The snow will fall
And all the creatures,
Big and small,
Will hibernate.

When winter comes,
The rain will pour
And wet the ground,
More and
More.

When winter comes,
Jack Frost is about
And freezes everything,
Inside and
Out.

When winter's end is finally here,
Most people give a cheer,
But I think winter's great,
We'll see it next year, I can't wait!

Laura Lee (10)
St Bride's Primary School

THE TENNIS MATCH

The two players came out of the gloom
One to win and one to his doom
In their white shirts and tanned skin
The match is just about to begin

We put our bags down by the chair
Giving each other a determined stare
We are waiting for the umpire's call
Impatient racquets want the ball

Out on the court we start the game
It's hard to choose, we look the same
Frantically slipping and sliding about
At every good shot the crowd will shout

'Game, set and match!' the umpire cries
The winner throws his racquet high
I'm ready now without a doubt
Tim Henman had better watch out!

Christopher Kinney (10)
St Bride's Primary School

HOMEWORK

Every day when I come home
The dreaded moment and then a moan
Oh why can I not just relax and watch TV
Much more beneficial to me
Then my mum checks with me
The homework diary, so she can see
What has been assigned to me on another faithful day
Maths or maybe science or whatever come what may.

Benjamin Lee (10)
St Bride's Primary School

MY CAT, SPOT

I have a white cat
whose name is Spot.
Sometimes he's white
and sometimes he's not.
But whether he's white
or whether he's not,
there's a patch on his eye
that makes him Spot.

He chews the phone
and he bites a ball.
He doesn't care,
for a mouse at all.
He eats too much
and miaows a lot.
But I'm glad he's my cat,
My cat, Spot.

Ruaidhri Austin (10)
St Bride's Primary School

ANOTHER WORLD

In my dreams I sometimes go to another world
My other world is a secret place
No one knows where I am
Everything is free
There are unlimited supplies of everything we need
The countryside is full of birds and animals
I discovered a dodo
I wish my dreams would never end.

Michael Webb (10)
St Bride's Primary School

Primary 8

When I look around my class,
I see familiar faces.

In a few months' time,
New ones will take their places.

Six years and more we've spent together,
Through thick and thin and nasty weather.

It started back in '97,
A bunch of angels sent from Heaven.

We all grew up and found our way,
Teachers grew older, some have gone grey.

The bond between us grows even stronger,
I wish so much it would go on longer.

No matter what I face next year,
I won't look back without a tear.

Ronan Cullen (10)
St Bride's Primary School

Snow

One day when it was snowing,
I started jumping with glee,
I went out and played all day
And I didn't come in till tea,
After tea I went out but all the
Snow had melted,
I went back in but with a grin.

Kevin Martin (10)
St Bride's Primary School

Lil' Sister Rap

Hip-hop, hip-hop, hap
This is my little sister rap

She drives me nuts, she takes my things
She steals my CDs and tries to sing

Hip-hop, hip-hop, hap
This is my little sister rap

She cries a lot, she wrecks my bed
All of this is doin' in my head

Hip-hop, hip-hop, hap
This is my little sister rap

My mum and dad think she's really gentle
But I think they must be mental
The teachers think she's really cool
Cos she acts a goody-two-shoes, when she's at school

Hip-hop, hip-hop, hap
This is my little sister rap

Those of you who've got sisters too
Must know what I'm going through
In spite of this, I really love her
As much as I love my father and mother

Hip-hop, hip-hop, hap
Hope you liked my
Little sister rap!

Anna Kerr (10)
St Bride's Primary School

MY FAMILY

My family are weirdoes,
They come from planet Zonk,
They all have a different special way
Of indicating what planet they're from.

My sister, she's probably the worst,
All pink and frilly cuffs,
Oh gossip, glory, gorgeous and girls,
She depends on pink and drives me nuts.

My brother has a brain of mush,
Zap, whizz, whizz, kabblamo!
He devours over games and PlayStations
And to think I even had a go.

My mum is pretty perfect,
Dirt is her worst enemy,
She embarrasses me in public,
Cleaning small snippets of dirt.

My dad is completely ga-ga,
He acts as if he's twelve (he wishes),
All football boys and smart remarks,
He plays it in the park (nightmare).

Now that's my family,
Father, Mother, sister, brother, but not me,
I'm just normal, regular in size,
Friends coming round for tea, but I am surprised and I can't deny,
How I didn't turn out like them.

Emma Johnson (10)
St Bride's Primary School

THE KING OF THE SKY

Oh feathered friend
I'd love to fly
Beside you
In the clear blue sky

We'd be great mates
As we stalk our prey
Some unsuspecting pigeon
Would have its day!

As we swoop at speed
With talons wide
We glide through the sky
Full of pride

After our fun
Tired and weary
We return once more
To our cosy eerie.

Eoin Kelly (10)
St Bride's Primary School

HOMEWORK

School drives me up the wall,
Homework is the worst of all,
Maths, English, science too,
Homework, homework, what's the point?
It makes us cry and hurts our arms,
Six hours of school and an extra long homework too,
Give us a break from work, work, work,
It will be less for us and less for you!

Nadine Quinn (10)
St Bride's Primary School

JINGLE BELLS

Jingle bells, babies yell
Dimitrios is such a drag
Miss Murphy's girls have flipped their curls
And Burns is such hag

Jingle bells, Michael tells
Little kids scream!
What's that? Oh, it's only the boys
For lunch they ate some beans

Jingle bells, Christmas bells
Two weeks off from school
Library books and cafeteria cooks
The holidays are cool!

Muhadasaeh Suhail (10)
St Bride's Primary School

THE SECRET CUPBOARD

I know a secret cupboard
Where deadly dragons hide
And when I'm feeling brave
I take a peep inside
To see a deadly dragon
With a hundred gleaming teeth
And eyes the size of apple pies
And four enormous feet
But should that deadly dragon
Turn his head my way
I'd shut the secret cupboard door
And run a mile away!

Catherine Blaney (10)
St Bride's Primary School

DREAMING OF THE CITY

As I sit in my bedroom
I look out the window, what do I see?
I see trees, nothing but trees
With my head in my hands, I glance at my knees
As I lift my head up, something catches my eye
It's glittery and sparkly and hanging up high
As I move my head closer, it becomes clear
It's a picture of a fairy I painted last year

I thought to myself
What would it be like to live in the city?
I never stop dreaming of bright lights and shops, what a pity
I know it is just a dream
But I still wish it was real.

Marie Finnegan (10)
St Bride's Primary School

GOLF

I love playing on a course
When you hit the ball with such force
I hate it when you shout, 'Fore!'
Because it affects your load roar

Once I got it in the hole
Then out popped a tiny mole
Once I hit it out of bounds
And won myself 10 whole pounds!

Then the captain said to me,
'We've never seen someone hit past that tree'
I don't like this game anymore
Because of the big loud 'Fore!'

Brendan Ferguson (10)
St Bride's Primary School

Winter

I look up at the tiny bits of fluffy candyfloss
As they float down to the ground
To make a carpet of white

I watch one of my neighbours attempting to get her car up the hill
But with no such luck

I see children slipping on the glossy ice rink
Wrapped up warm like little Eskimos
Having lots of fun

Birds are soaring through the sky on a long journey south
While other animals are tucked up warm on a bed of frosty leaves

Winter is my special season
It makes me feel at home
There's just something magical about it.

Katie Clarke (10)
St Bride's Primary School

Friday At Three

On Friday when the clock strikes three
Everyone is as happy as can be
Miss Murphy says, 'Pack up your books,'
We're already through the door, no backward looks

Outside we're free, my mates and me
And very soon the school we flee
But then it's all over far too soon
And it is so long from Monday to Friday afternoon.

Patrick Fee (10)
St Bride's Primary School

THE BULLY

She's waiting for me by the gate,
She looks up and says, 'You're late.'
I cannot tell her name,
She sounds it, but she's not tame.
She pushes me against the bars,
People look from passing cars.

I cannot tell my mum or dad,
'Cause that would make her really mad
Or if I tell a teacher or two,
She'll flush my head right down the loo!
She does this every single day,
Stealing my lunch money in her evil way.

When she calls someone a horrible name,
She says, 'It was her, Miss,' and I get the blame.
I haven't had a good play time in one whole year,
For when I go outside, I'm full of fear,
She makes me do her homework as well as my own,
No one will stand up for me, I'm all alone.

This little missy has gone way too far,
Calling me names for going around in 'Daddy's posh car'.
'Teacher's pet,' I always hear,
From she who got an 'A' when we wrote about King Lear.
She obviously has never met
My big sis, Cat,
Who will teach her a lesson she'll never forget!

Jennifer Wright (10)
St Bride's Primary School

DRAGON POEM

Dragon, dragon, mighty beast,
Fire-breathing mouth
And gruesome teeth,
Red, blue, yellow and green,
These are the colours of his skin
And spotty dots all over him,
With his big dark eyes
You can't see him watching you,
Watching you, watching you
And then he jumps and kills you.

Aoibhe McCann (10)
St Bride's Primary School

THE SNOW

It snowed last night,
The ground went white,
So we all ran out
For a snowball fight,
My toes were frozen,
My bum went numb,
The snow hit me like
It came out of a gun,
I ran and ran
Until I ran too far,
Then ran back to base
To continue the chase,
After a while
I could take it no more,
My fingers were sore,
So I headed straight for the door!

Kevin Scott (10)
St Bride's Primary School

MY BEST FRIEND

I have a best friend you know,
We're always on the go,
We play and play every day,
We swap each other's work,
We go to the shops and buy ice cream,
Chocolate, strawberry, raspberry and vanilla,
We eat them with the hot sun burning over our heads,
Life is great, best friends forever,
We sit together and watch Tracy Beaker,
We laugh and laugh until we barf,
We have sleepovers and try and try and
Find out about each other's futures in magazines,
We go to designer stores and pick out tops
For the disco at school,
We don't eat egg otherwise we're sick,
We rather prefer candy sticks,
We annoy our mothers for pocket money,
To buy our Mizz magazines,
We stand in the shop for ages looking at the gossip,
We go to kids' stores and look at the dolls,
Finally we get the bus home,
We sing songs on the CD player,
Our favourite tune, 'Cry Me A River' by Justin Timberlake,
I reach home hugging and greeting my best friend,
Goodbye, it's been a fun day,
My best friend is the greatest,
I understand her, she understands me, forever we'll be.

Candice Robinson (10)
St Bride's Primary School

A Winter Walk

I went for a walk through the frosty fields,
With the cold wind nipping my face,
I don't want to be late for tea,
So I have to quicken my pace.

I lean over the wall to see
Some happy faces watching me,
Others are skating on the ice,
Believe me, I think it's nice!

The moon reflecting in the pond,
Sending shadows across the lawn,
I can't wait to sit down to dinner,
On a lovely winter's night!

Mary Carson (8)
St Bride's Primary School

The Eye Of The Tiger

The striking shadow shifts through the night,
And then . . . within a striking moment a frightening flash
                                                        of an orange light,
A brave soul appears with a dashing strike,
Tiger, tiger in the night, burning oh so bright,
Now the fearsome monster eats violently,
With a carnivorous soul, a fearsome-looking mouth,
Tiger, tiger in the night, burning oh so bright,
Now the carnivorous creature is sleepy,
It sleeps fearsomely and loudly,
But drifts to sleep sweetly and silently,
Tiger, tiger in the night, burning oh so bright.

Gavin McGranaghan (8)
St Bride's Primary School

TIDYING MY ROOM

First I made a secret passage under my bed,
I made up my password,
Pick any number under forty
Then add or subtract to give yourself an answer of thirty,
No more or no less.

If you are scared of the dark,
You might not come out alive!
Say the password *Ghost-Kong*
To switch the rope light on.

I go under my table, at the entrance to my secret tunnel,
I push a box forward,
I keep the box with me at all times
So no burglars (girls) can get under there
And steal my secret plans.

My Mogwai toy gives me the task sheet,
Take the toys out from under the bed
And put them in their proper place, is the task to be done,
Now seven times repeat,
Until the mission is complete.

Stephen McKeever (8)
St Bride's Primary School

Football Crazy

I'm crazy about football,
I bet you're not as crazy as me,
I'm going to see Man U play in March,
When they score I'll shout, 'Yippee!'

I'm going to get one of their shirts
And have 'Prenter' on the back,
So when I return home,
I'll hit the ball in the back of the net!

When I'm back at school,
I'll bring my ball into the yard,
So when Peter tries to score some goals,
I'll save them easy, not hard.

After I come home from school,
I think I'll call for my friends
And invite them all to my house,
To play football till the day ends!

Donal Prenter (8)
St Bride's Primary School

Armagh

On the 22nd of September
In the year of 2002
We went to Dublin on the orange choo-choo
They scored a few goals
And had lots of fun!
And my goodness they did run!
And by the end, they won!

Tom Dowling (8)
St Bride's Primary School

THE STREAM OF DIAMONDS

One day as I went out to play,
I thought to go the other way,
I went across a bridge,
But as I looked down I could see,
A stream of diamonds beneath me.

As the grasshopper and the frogs sang their songs,
The stream of diamonds started to dance,
To me, this was a delight,
Until it came to morning light,
Then the singing stopped
And the stream no longer glistened,
As it listened
And danced in the moonlight.

Amy Doran (8)
St Bride's Primary School

THE SNOWFLAKE

It was like a twirling star
You wouldn't notice it from afar
It was gazing in the night
So beautiful and bright
Such a wonderful sight

It looked like a dazzling light
It was all silvery and white
As it glowed in the ebony night
It felt all slushy
And a bit too mushy
It seemed all soft and cold
And it looked like the story
Was about to unfold.

Charley Morrison (8)
St Bride's Primary School

WINTER MAGIC

As I walked down the slippery street
Full of ice and snow
I looked at a *big* clump of ice
And said a great big *wow!*
I looked at a car window
And saw all of the pictures
That Jack Frost had drawn
And he just there seemed to say
'I'll draw one of you!'
I thought of my house
With a nice warm fire
And on that very cold day
I would like to have done
While eating a nice warm scone!

Conall Cahill (8)
St Bride's Primary School

WEATHER POEM

The wind and rain
Spoil my fun
The snow and hail
Are very cold
On the other hand
The sun is roasting warm
The worst of all is the rain
It is boring
I can't go out to play
But oh how I love the snow
I build a snowman
We have a snowball fight.

James Gildea (8)
St Bride's Primary School

SUMMER

Summer days, lie-ins in bed,
No school to annoy my sleepy head.
Up for breakfast, think about the day,
Friends, swim, sunbathe, play, play, play!

I take my neighbour's dog Archie for a walk,
Meet my friends for an ice cream and talk.
All the family drive to the beach,
Scored a goal against my brother, what a peach!

Go shopping with Mum to buy some clothes,
Read a book in the sun, then a little doze,
Relaxing day, a scrumptious dinner, dishes a chore,
Watch a film, snuggle in bed, snore, snore!

Planning our holiday, we're off to France,
New friends to meet, cloudy weather, not a chance!
Cycle around the campsite, swim at the pool,
Not a teacher in sight enforcing the rule.

Jane Kelly (8)
St Bride's Primary School

SUMMER

The sun burning on my chest
Ice cream melting down my cheek
Sprinkler splashing everywhere
Flowers blooming in the soil
Grass prickling on my feet
The school bell ringing for the last time
All you hear is, 'It's summer! It's summer!'

Michael Loughrey (8)
St Bride's Primary School

SNOW

Ah! What a wonderful morning!
The sun has risen but Dad's still snoring!
I look out the window and what do I see?
Some snowflakes and a snow-covered Christmas tree.
It's snowing and snowing on top of the ground,
Icicles are hanging from branches around.
Clear snow, bright snow, icy cold, starlit snow.
I pull on my hat, my gloves and a scarf.
Hoping Dad has left the fire on in the hearth.

What a wonderful feeling,
I feel as tall as our twelve foot ceiling!
There is my snowman made of crystal clear snow
And my sister's made a princess with some buttons and a bow.

But the next day I moan and I groan,
Mum says, 'Stop complaining!'
But I can't - it's raining!

Lara Smyth (9)
St Bride's Primary School

WINTER STORM

The storm was deep, deep and dark,
Hailstones falling very hard,
You could see it coming full of fear,
Coming close and very near.

When I went to bed that night,
I woke up with a terrible fright,
Then I realised what a wonderful sight,
The snow was falling, soft and white.

Sophie Trainor (8)
St Bride's Primary School

RAIN

Rain, rain, rain
Down my cheek
It feels like I've won
The rain-winning streak
I splash in the puddles
Soaking my feet
Rain, rain, rain trickling
Down my cheek

Rain, rain, rain trickling
Down my cheek
I like spring showers
When the baby lambs bleat
But when the sun
Dries all the rain
This is when I
Wait for the
Rain again.

Lianna Dalmeny (9)
St Bride's Primary School

RAINY DAYS

The raindrops keep falling on my head
The rain was splashing on the ground
So I'll have to run instead
I went to sleep that night
I woke up that morning
The rain had stopped
I went outside but the rain
Came splashing back on again
So I had to go inside.

Nicholas Ferguson (8)
St Bride's Primary School

SUPER SEASONS

The rainbows are flying
The sun is burning
The sunshine is dazzling hot
This is the season of summer.
It's a misty dark morning
The smooth feel of snow is touching my face
The snow is falling down
It's not polluted, just very clean
This is the season of winter.
Gushing, rustling, splashing down
The rain is hitting my head
The days are wet, cold and mild
Droplets are falling from a high sky
This is the season of autumn.
The cloudless sky is shining
Flowers are starting to bloom
Daffodils are growing
Birds are singing peacefully
This is the season of spring.

John O'Neill (9)
St Bride's Primary School

THE FOREST

The forest is dark
Because it's full of trees
I can hear dogs bark
And see honeybees
I ran out of the forest and out of the dark
Because I'd rather be playing in the park.

Finn McKenna (9)
St Bride's Primary School

SUMMER

Autumn, winter, spring, it makes me want to sing,
But summer is the best, at least that's what I think.
Beaches and donkey rides and fat, juicy peaches,
Suncream and swimsuits and spades
And waves that sound like blasting grenades.

As the sun is beating on my back,
It's like it's saying, 'Come on, don't slack!'
The top of the waves look like dancing white horses,
But collapse as they fall when they take their different courses.

I feel sad as I get into the car,
To go away, go away, go away far.
To leave all the sunshine and summer behind,
To see teachers and work and lessons galore,
I wish I could be back on the seashore.

Orla Herity (9)
St Bride's Primary School

WHEN THE SUN WAS MEAN TO ME

It was a cold winter's morning,
I was sitting in my class,
When all of a sudden the sun rose up,
Melting winter's grasp
And when school was over,
I could finally jump in the snow,
But to my surprise,
I could not believe my eyes,
The snow was gone,
Gone, gone, gone . . .

Jack McCann (9)
St Bride's Primary School

SUMMER

Summertime is lots of fun
I get to play out in the sun
I go to the beach
Get ice cream
Put on my swimsuit
And go down to the sea

I come out of the sea
Freezing cold
Then, when I put a towel round me
I'm warm, dry and cosy

After that I sunbathe
I get so comfortable
That I fall asleep
The only thing that spoils my dream
Is the dreaded bottle of *suncream!*

Fiona Hunt (9)
St Bride's Primary School

THE WEATHER

Rainy days are always boring
I'd like to go outside
But Mum says no, so I can't go
Until it starts to snow

Sunny days are always fun
Especially when it's just begun
I hate it when the clouds come out
Because it teases the sun about.

Rebecca Carr (9)
St Bride's Primary School

SEASONS

Weather poems are seasonal,
Spring, summer, autumn and winter,
Which do you like best?
Please do be reasonable!

Spring has lambs and budding flowers,
Summer, we escape school and play for hours,
My dad loves walking in autumn leaves,
But he is very hard to please!

Howling wind and frosty morn,
Wrap up tight before the storm,
Santa, snowmen, garden robins and frozen ponds,
Cheers me to ignore the rest,
Winter is the season I love best.

Olivia McCauley (9)
St Bride's Primary School

A WINTER'S DAY

Slipping, sliding, skidding too,
On the ice, that's what I do,
It's cold and gentle but do watch out,
There may be snowballs all about.

One, two, three, four,
I want there to be lots more,
Snowflakes falling down and down,
Will they ever reach the ground?

Lying there in a bed of snow,
Being covered from head to toe,
The sun comes out and there it stays,
It melts all our fun away.

Nainsi McKernan (9)
St Bride's Primary School

THE HORRORS OF THE WORLD

The world is such a murderous plot.
Dying, dying, dying every day.
Like a wounded stag,
It suffers most intensely.

But this is not the world's fault.
There are many suspects here,
But really the most guilty is money,
A dismay.

There is murder,
There is death,
Starvation and the rest,
But money is to really blame.

You need money to buy weapons,
A dead human leaves a will.
Starvation wouldn't be the same,
For money which buys our grain.

Filthy, filthy, money.

Beulah McGeachie (9)
St Bride's Primary School

WINTER POEM

I ran outside to see the snow,
The twinkling snowflakes falling so slow,
It looks like a snowflake dancing in the air,
We all turn around to stop and stare,
The crunching of the snow and the wind in my face
And the footsteps in the snow that we like to trace.

Anna Maguire (9)
St Bride's Primary School

CANDYFLOSS SNOW

I woke one day
What did I see?
A blanket of snow all over the garden
There was snow on my window sill
Twinkling down

I wanted to eat it
It was like candyfloss
It was delicate, eloquent
Quite silvery

It felt all mushy and slushy
It started to melt, oh no!
It was cold and tickly
Then all gone, melted by the sun.

Megan O'Hare (9)
St Bride's Primary School

SNOWFLAKES

Snowflakes fall gently to the ground,
Snowflakes fall without making a sound,
They twirl and swirl in the air,
They land on trees that are bare,
Snowflakes fall in many ways,
But they're only here for a few days,
They're so soft, like candyfloss,
It's nice to see them swirl in the sky,
Some are low, some are high,
Once you feel a tickly spike,
They become the best thing you like!

Melissa Timoney (9)
St Bride's Primary School

A Snowdrop

A small white snowdrop, lonely as can be,
See it waving in the wind on the hillside,
A bright-red rose coming over to see,
A dazzling little bee carrying over some honey,
All sit down and have a chocolate bunny,
Now on the hill early in the morning,
The sun comes up, the sky is dawning,
The small little snowdrop started to grow,
He became as big as a gigantic sunflower,
Now he's in the mood to go and play,
When the iciness came over the hillside,
The large white snowdrop started to say,
When I die in the springtime,
Lots of me will start to grow again.

Emma Quinn (9)
St Bride's Primary School

Expressions

My brother wears odd expressions
Screwed-up as can be
My friends wear happy expressions
Joyful as can be
My mother wears posh expressions
Showy as can be
My father wears tired expressions
Weary as can be
My teacher wears clever expressions
Brainy as can be
And two, like the cat and dog
Indescribable as can be.

Rachel Connolly (9)
St Bride's Primary School

SNOWFLAKES

Snowflakes falling to the ground
Swirling, twirling round and round
Dancing, prancing all around me
A dead white blanket lying on the ground
Falling down without a sound

It's white and silvery
And it's very bright
It's elegantly spiky
They're soft, white and fluffy little clouds

Sometimes it can be mushy
But yet again it can be slushy
Get your snowballs ready to throw
I like playing in the snow.

Patrick Short (9)
St Bride's Primary School

HOMEWORK

Homework is such a pest
So give us all a rest

Even though you might like it
We don't, it's one thing we detest

If you don't want to give it to us
Yes, you're the best

We hate it if it is a test
One wee sum, that's the best

I know all teachers will not agree, including Mr D
But I am still only a child,
Someday I might be on your side.

Colette Duffy (9)
St Bride's Primary School

CAN MY BIRTHDAY GET ANY WORSE?

Here comes the cake
The one that I hate
It's been set on the table
The one that's unstable
Can my birthday get any worse?

My friends have come
But there's only one
Can my birthday be any fun?

Granny bought me a football
And some boots as well
I tried to tell her, I'm a girl

After that my mum did bring
The biggest thing I'd ever seen

It's a bike, as big as can be
So my birthday's not so bad
Wouldn't you agree?

Kate O'Hara (9)
St Bride's Primary School

FOOTIE RULES!

Footie rules are hard and severe,
Ref shouts, 'Don't touch that sphere!'
Yellow or red card if you kick someone down
Or score a goal and receive a crown!

Score a goal and receive attention
Or fight with the ref and get detention!
Or actually be the ref, sharp as a thistle,
Know all the footie rules and blow the whistle!

Tony Stow (9)
St Bride's Primary School

MY FAMILY TREE

One's small
One's tall and
One's in-between

And then, well of course
There's me
But wait, don't go,
There's more to know
About my family tree

There's aunts and uncles
Cousins too
There's also grannies
And grandads
And that's all
Thank goodness!

Mary Kervick (8)
St Bride's Primary School

WINTER

Oh, winter snow creeps in like a quiet stranger,
It falls silently and gently during the night,
It's such a fright to see this wonderful sight.
When I wake up, I look out to see a red robin on the shed,
Looking silently back at me.
We are both surprised by the soft, glistening blanket of white snow,
The garden is a new white wonderful world,
Everything is magical.
I take a deep breath, I cannot wait to go outside and explore,
This crystal white enchanting land.

Lauren McLaughlin (9)
St Bride's Primary School

THE WINTER ROBIN

Sitting on my window sill
I heard the sweetest sound
It was a robin
But not just any robin
A winter robin was its name
He was now flying round
It's obvious he was getting warm
Because it was very, very cold
Looking out the window
The flakes were starting to fall
I was worried about the winter robin
So I tried and tried to call
It came in through the opening
But it flew on down the stairs
The robin was near the fire
I knew he wanted to stay
Very sad, I knew someday
I'd have to say goodbye.

Orla Gormley (8)
St Bride's Primary School

ODE TO ICE CREAM

Ice cream, ice cream
I like you a lot
You keep me cool
When the day is hot
You're tasty and delicious
You're also nutritious
Your flavours are the best
That I have got, better than the rest!

Mark Salters (9)
St Bride's Primary School

SWEETS

Sweets are good
Sweets are fun
Sweets are fun for everyone

They may be yummy
They may be nice
Because they're made from sugar and spice

There are chocolate ones
There are fruity ones
They are a kid's delight

But remember to brush your teeth
Before you say
Goodnight.

Jade Zemrowsky (9)
St Bride's Primary School

SPORT

The thing I love most is sport
I love sports of every sort
Football, swimming, tennis or hockey
I would even like to ride a horse as a jockey

Doing sports makes us fit and healthy
It even makes some people very wealthy
David Beckham is an example of one sport's star
He's even bought his baby son a brand new car

So when I grow up, my dream is to be
The thing that is really important to me
A footballer like Becks and Owen
And maybe the best the world's ever known!

John Kerr (9)
St Bride's Primary School

A Winter's Day

The evergreen tree stands alone
Most birds are not at home
The robin stands alone

The migrating birds
They do not know
What the robin thinks of snow

The snow falls to the ground
Making very little sound
The evergreen tree stands so mighty
As the snow is played very happily

The evergreen tree
Taller than most
Is indeed the snowball fight host

The robin
Flies around
Looking for any food upon the ground
That is a tale of a winter's day
That is all I can say.

Conor McGowan (9)
St Bride's Primary School

My Mum

My mum does all the cooking
My mum does all the tidying
And she makes things shining
She has to stop all the whining
When she is going shopping
And she is very loving
So that is my mum.

Ben Leonard (9)
St Bride's Primary School

Getting Married

You're getting married hip, hip, hooray
I'm sure you will look beautiful on your wedding day
Carrots and parsnips, other vegetables too
People smiling and waving at you
Sit at a huge table you and the others
Sit with your sisters, sit with your brothers
Mummy and Daddy smiling and weeping
People with cameras looking and peeping
Here comes the cake, but it's not a fake
Out in the garden runs a long lake
Go on, make a speech
But don't sing or screech
Just think of your honeymoon and the lovely white beach
There will be lots of dancing, music and prancing
Your friends will all be laughing and glancing
But last is the kiss, which we wouldn't miss
The whole room goes silent, just think of the bliss
Now the day's over, everyone has had fun
Now the day's over
Now the day's done.

Eimear McDonnell (9)
St Bride's Primary School

My Dog

I have a Jack Russell who's always in trouble,
She follows me to school,
One day in the spring,
She learnt how to sing,
While following me to school.
The teacher near cried out loud with surprise,
On hearing my doggy sing.

Ruairi Fallon McGuigan (9)
St Bride's Primary School

IF WE HAD ONE MORE

In my family
There's my mum, dad and me
I wish we had one more
But if it was a boy
Guess what?
He'd be fighting
All the time
With his older sister
Me
If it was a girl
Her name would be Pearl
I'd like her a lot
And I'd help her do dot-to-dot
If it was twins
They would be out of the house
In no time at all
Because . . .
I wouldn't stand the
Noise
So thankfully
In my family
There's just my mum, dad and
Me.

Sorcha Foster (9)
St Bride's Primary School

SITTING ON THE GARAGE ROOF

Sitting on the garage roof,
I'm in big trouble now.
The cup fell and broke itself -
And I'm having a row.

I don't know how to escape from here,
My ball smashed through the door.
Mum is really angry now,
I'm sure I'll get an extra chore.

I didn't break the computer,
It was like that when I came in.
How was I supposed to know -
The keys were in the bin!

I think I should say sorry,
Besides, I want my tea.
Forgive me everybody
And help me down this tree!

Aedin O'Kane (9)
St Bride's Primary School

DOGS!

Dogs can run and jump all day,
They are always eager for a play.

When it is time for a bath, they always run,
They don't think it's any fun.

They love attention and lots of fuss
And they get that from all of us.

They're covered in fur, but make a great friend
And will always stick with you to the very end!

Alice Keenan (10)
St Bride's Primary School

MR FROST

Mr Frost is in the garden,
He leaves a sparkly blanket,
It's like a crystal banquet.
The grass is hard,
The pond is frozen
And the ducks are slipping,
Upon the icy pond,
It's like an icy mirror.
My sister and I,
Love to play and watch,
The glistening icicles drop from
The mossy drainpipes.

Rory Flanagan (9)
St Bride's Primary School

NIGHT

I look out my window in the night
I sit and wonder at the sight
Of twinkling stars like tiny lights
That brighten up this cold dark night

The scaredy-cat is on the prowl
For little creatures that escape the owl
They hide in boxes in the street
And nibble on old shredded wheat

I imagine to be out on the cold, gloomy night
And think that Jack Frost might come and bite
He might bite my cold toes
Or even my runny nose
Who next will he bite?
My brother I suppose.

Katherine O'Boyle (9)
St Bride's Primary School

SNOW

As I was walking in the snow
I saw a robin on my bow
I put it down upon a bush
And walked back home through the slush

I passed a house that was covered with snow
A little girl was outside and her name was Jo
We played together her and I
Making a snowman, oh so high!

We saw a sparrow with snow on her head
She looked very cold and wanted a warm bed
So up she flew to her nest above
And snuggled in beside a dove

We said goodbye
And went back home
And sat down by the fire
To write a winter poem!

Méabh McHugh-Hill (9)
St Bride's Primary School

FOOTBALL

Once upon a time on the pitch,
One of the players fell in a ditch!
He had had a clear shot on goal,
I bet he hates that darn mole!

The match it ended 3-2
And his team did not go through!
From this day on and maybe later,
He will be a mole exterminator!

Ben Johnston (10)
St Bride's Primary School

VAN IS THE MAN

He is like lightning
All the defenders think he is frightening

The crowd call him Ruud
Because he never gets booed

I think he is shrewd
Because he's a cool dude

He has scored 52 goals
Set up mostly by Scholes

It is without a doubt that Van is the man
And does all he can to beat West Ham

He is Ruud Van Nistelrooy of
Manchester United.

Garrett Cullen (9)
St Bride's Primary School

MY BIG SISTER

My big sister thinks she's grand
She plays an instrument in a rock band
She prances off to school each day
Smiling at the boys on her way

She says she has to work so hard
But all she does, it seems to me
Is dance and eat and watch TV

When I grow up, I'll surely be
So very different, just wait and see!

Ellen Gordon (9)
St Bride's Primary School

A Family

Do you have a brother? Yes,
Does he make a mess?
Brothers are really very rude,
But when your mum comes in, they are good.

Do you like your sister? No,
I didn't really expect so.
Is she nice to your best friend?
If yes, then your hair would stand on end.

Does your mum annoy you sometimes?
Like when she tries to feed you limes.
Does she send you to your room
To be in the room of doom?

Does your dad support Man U?
If he doesn't, shout *boo*.
Does he really love his food?
I'd say yes, as all dads do.

Well, that's a family belonging to someone,
So would you like to have one?

Beth McMullan (9)
St Bride's Primary School

THE SNAKE I'VE SEEN

The snake I've seen
Squirms and slithers
Sometimes it gives me the shivers
It doesn't talk much
Apart from a hiss
I can't really explain
All of this
Well that's all I've heard
And it even tried to eat my bird
The snake I've seen is
Very green
Brown, yellow and shiny
The snake I've seen
Is nowhere to be seen
Oh crikey!

Lucy Southern (10)
St Bride's Primary School

THE SWAN

The swan glides gracefully
Through the sky
Its beautiful silver wings
Flowing past
Then it lands
In the water elegantly
The swan's beautiful body
Glides into the deep blue water
And then the swan swims
Into the golden sunset.

Sarah McLernon (9)
St Bride's Primary School

School

School is boring,
School is unfair,

I bet you would not like,
To spend the day there,

School is nerve-racking,
When you are doing a test,
But I have not told you,
The worst bit yet,

You get in through the gates
And you get into line,
Then your teacher comes out
And asks, 'Are you all fine?'

Everyone in the line will reply,
'Of course I am, Miss,
Why shouldn't I?'

I only joke however, I only jest,
My teacher is the very best!

Paula Moloney (9)
St Bride's Primary School

WARHAMMER

Warhammer is my hobby,
I love it so much,
The figures I collect
Are Lord of the Rings,
From Strider to the Balrog,
I'm collecting a good few,
I paint them then battle,
Sometimes I win, sometimes I lose,
My best friend in school collects it too,
His favourite is Empire,
He's got quite a few.

Joshua O'Hagan (9)
St Bride's Primary School

MY LITTLE BROTHER

I have a little brother
Who's really like no other
He's fair and tall
Whereas I am small
He's only four
And at teatime always asks for more
He really loves his food
And is seldom ever rude
When I go to sleep in bed
He always wants to get fed
At night he plays with his lorry
I say, 'Stop and I'll read you a story.'
He may sometimes be a little pest
But I think he is simply the best.

Caelan Rush (9)
St Bride's Primary School

THE CAT WHO PLAYED THE PLAYSTATION

My mum bought me a PlayStation
Oh, what a fantastic creation!
It's shiny and black
Just like my cat
But I've told him it's *my* PlayStation!
I came home unexpectedly one day
I'm not sure, but I think it was in May
And what did I see
But my cat, Zachary
Playing my PlayStation
Like crazy!

Conall Forker (9)
St Bride's Primary School

ON A WINTER DAY

On a winter day
We decided to play
On the blistering snow
Which was on its own

The snow was thick and white
The place was bright in the light
And we had a snowball fight

We made a snowman
And gave him a hat
And we named him Pat.

Iswarya Kalyan (9)
St Bride's Primary School

TEENAGE BROTHER

My brother doesn't wash his face
His hair is never trim
My brother's not afraid of germs
But they're afraid of him

All he eats is cake and sweets
And fails to brush his teeth
He wears his socks inside out
And always finds something to shout about

But that's my brother
And I'm proud of him.

Matt McClean (9)
St Bride's Primary School

WINTER FEELINGS

Winter is dark and as cold as can be
It's a time for thinking of people unlike me
At least I have a fire and a cosy bed
While others are cold and think what lies ahead

Children have fun playing in the snow
While others think different and wish it would go
Because they are sad and want a home
They also want a family for they feel alone

So when you're as snug, as snug as can be
Think of those people unlike you and me!

Chloe MacAuley (10)
St Bride's Primary School

THE WINTER WEATHER WATCH

One day I saw a slinky cat,
Walking down the street,
As snow was laying on the ground,
It really was quite bleak.

It was falling down one by one,
All white and soft as fluff,
It was really quite a shame,
When it melted in the sun.

Even when it rained,
The snow was still around,
Filling Belfast with a gleam,
Not making any sound.

They came in little tiny balls,
Oh how sweet to see,
Some were very icy,
Some were very nice to eat,
I liked the way they all came down
And filled me with such glee.

Sometimes snow doesn't come,
How sad can it be?
But I believe that snow brings joy,
Just for you and me,
So come out, enjoy the fun,
With the snow, you and me.

Katie Campbell (9)
St Bride's Primary School

My TV

My TV is a big brown box
It's very big and it rocks

It's got two hundred channels
Some are very good
Sometimes I watch them when I'm eating my food

My favourite channel is Sky One
It has The Simpsons
They're great fun
Spider-Man is super cool
Sabrina makes me drool
Goosebumps gives me the frights
I wouldn't watch it at night

Even though it may rain
It would drive me insane
But I have TV
Sometimes it makes me sad
Sometimes it makes me mad
But most of all makes me glad
Because I have TV.

Odhran Burke (9)
St Bride's Primary School

MY DOG, LYNN

I've got a dog called Lynn,
As soon as she's out, she wants back in,
I don't know what to do with her!

When she's in,
She tears down the house,
But when she's out,
She ruins the flower beds
And Mum gets really cross,
I don't know what to do with her!

Maybe I should give her away
Or maybe I should give her to Auntie Jane
Or maybe not, I think I'll keep her,
Because she's my little Lynn!

Ellen McGrath (9)
St Bride's Primary School

CAN YOU PLAY FOOTBALL?

Can you kick a ball up high?
Can you header it into the sky?
Can you dribble with your left and right foot?
Can you take a corner so that your teammate can score?
Can you do the style just like Roy Keane?
Can you whack the ball so it can't be seen?
Can you skim a lot of players just like Ruud van Nistelrooy?
Can you bend it like Beckham?

Aoife Montague (10)
St Bride's Primary School

THE SNOW

The snow, the snow,
Us kids love the snow.
Our faces get oh so red, they even glow,
We build snowmen and have a snowball fight
And even give our mum a fright.

The snow-covered buildings and land,
Make us feel good and look so grand.
We really do love the snow you know,
We hope and pray that you know.

Our mum we think does not like the snow,
'The washing, the washing,' she says,
'I hope the snow will soon go.'
But we have lots of fun each day
And hope the snow will always stay.

Alas, the snow has nearly gone
And we are feeling very sad,
But we should think of brighter days,
With our memories of the snow all gone.

Rachael Rainey (9)
St Bride's Primary School

MY SECRET

Do you want to know my secret
About a little smell?
Do you want to know my secret?
Promise not to tell
Come closer, come closer
No, even closer
My secret is - not telling you!

Conor Donnelly (8)
St John The Baptist Boys' Primary School

MY CAT, MOLLY

Molly! Molly! Molly! She is very jolly
She's our little cat
And she's definitely not fat
She runs about the house
Hunting for a mouse

When she goes outside
She always tries to hide
In a little tree
To see what she can see

She makes sure she can't be heard
By the little bird
She's young, fierce and hungry
But never very scared

When she needs to rest her head
She goes to her little bed
And stays there to have a sleep
And all her dreams to keep.

Liam Williams (10)
St John The Baptist Boys' Primary School

MY FAMILY

My baby sister
Has tiny hands and feet
She has a little button nose
Which she never, never blows
Her hair stands up on her head
She never sleeps in her own bed
When I walk into the room
My baby sister smiles at me.

Aiden Cochrane (8)
St John The Baptist Boys' Primary School

THE KING OF ROCK

There once was a king
Who could really swing and sing
He had everything
Cash, cars, diamond rings

He had so many hits
He stacked them like bricks
When he made a hit
He got paid quite a bit

Elvis was his name
Singing was his game
Which gave him his fame
And that's how he became
The King of Rock and Roll

His music lives on in people today
Who try so hard to copy his way
But let them try
And let them be
'Cause there will only ever be
One *Elvis Presley.*

Conor Nugent (11)
St John The Baptist Boys' Primary School

CELTIC BOYS

The day I joined Celtic Boys
Was a day I made a lot of noise
It was always my wish
And it had finally come true
My daddy was proud
And I got new boots too.

Mark McKenna (9)
St John The Baptist Boys' Primary School

TREES

I think that I
Shall never see
A poem as lovely
As a tree

A tree that looks
At God all day
And lifts its leafy
Arms to pray

A tree that may
In summer wear
A nest of robins
In its hair

Poems are made by
Fools like me
But only God
Can make a tree.

Conor Willoughby (11)
St John The Baptist Boys' Primary School

MY DOG, HARVEY

Harvey is the name of my dog
He always loves to get wet
His ears reach down to the ground
He falls over them when he turns around
Harvey is black, white and brown
His face always has a frown
My dog's eyes look sad
But really he's quite mad.

Mark McCaffrey (8)
St John The Baptist Boys' Primary School

MY PET

I have a pet, a hairy one
His fur is golden, like the sun
He is full of fun

He stays up all night
And has a little bite
He is so sweet
And loves all his treats

He is so desirable
And really admirable
Clinging to the bars
He thinks it's a monkey bar

He is very noisy
As well as being nosy
It's just my little hamster
In its little hamper

Hairy Harry is his name.

Carlo Angelone (11)
St John The Baptist Boys' Primary School

OH HOW I WISH I WAS A POP STAR

Oh how I wish I was a big pop star
Like Will Young and Gareth Gates
With lists of hits that go on and on
I wish I was old enough to enter the show
With a mark of 10 out of 10
The judges would say, 'You're the best I've seen all day.'
And the crowd would cheer
Maybe someday I will be that big pop star.

Conal Sheppard (8)
St John The Baptist Boys' Primary School

THE LONDON STREETS

In the streets of London
Not a person to be seen
Now you can see that it
Is not very clean

It is winter now
And the snow is very thick
But is falling very quick
And the snow is as high as a cloud

It is now spring
And it is very clean
The birds are singing
And the chicks are yelling

It is early summer now
The sun is very bright
And with such light
People come out at night.

Matthew McPolin (11)
St John The Baptist Boys' Primary School

FISH

I have a pet, it is a fish
And it eats its dinner from a dish
When people said, 'Look at that!'
It said it even wears a hat
It swims round and round every day
And it has a special way of saying hey
My little fish can even roll over
And nowadays I call him Rover.

Eamann McDowell (8)
St John The Baptist Boys' Primary School

A POEM

Hello, I'm Kevin Shannon,
I am not tall,
I am small.

My favourite team is Liverpool,
I think all the players are cool.
My favourite animal is a cat,
You put money on it and that's a bet.

My nicest fruit is a pear,
I wish Gerry Adams was the mayor.
My favourite make is Nike,
I also have a BMX bike.

The worst thing is school,
The best thing is going to a swimming pool.
My favourite subject is PE,
My worst is geography.

Kevin Shannon (9)
St John The Baptist Boys' Primary School

MY HOUSE

My house is . . .
At the front of the street
With a strong front door with no curtains
Inside it's cold
Full of people shouting
Until Mum shouts, 'Bed children!'
Washed and in bed
When I watch TV
I fall asleep safely
In my house.

Ryan Willoughby (9)
St John The Baptist Boys' Primary School

SUMMER GOES

Summer goes, summer goes
Like the sand beneath my toes
But some days the strong wind blows
That's the way that summer goes

Summer, summer, it's always sunny
I like to watch the bees make honey
I like to watch the flowers grow
That's the way that summer goes

Summer goes, summer goes
I sneeze as winter freezes my nose
It's the time to wrap up warm
To sit at night and watch the storm.

Ryan Sewell (9)
St John The Baptist Boys' Primary School

MY HOBBIES

My hobbies are hurley and tennis,
But I also like Gaelic, it is good.
What about pool? It is great as well,
I love football because it is swell.
I like swimming, I like swimming a lot,
I also like playing golf,
There are lots of things for me to do.
I like playing the computer after school,
I want to play basketball or something like that,
Oh I like cycling and sometimes I run,
I love doing all of them, they're fun.

Niall Connolly (8)
St John The Baptist Boys' Primary School

BEVERLY HILLS

Beverly Hills, Beverly Hills, that's where I want to go
I want to go so bad I'm jumping with excitement
And I'm going crazy and mad,
Beverly Hills, Beverly Hills

The roads are crowded and busy
Everyone beeps the horn
They nearly knocked me down
Because I gave the driver a dirty frown
Beverly Hills, Beverly Hills

The buildings were huge, it was amazing
I'd never seen anything like it
It was bigger than the Twin Towers
The buildings were nearly up to the stars
Beverly Hills, Beverly Hills

The houses were beautiful
The nicest I've ever seen
Some of them were so glamorous
They were as nice as the twilight beam
Beverly Hills, Beverly Hills.

Colum Carroll (11)
St John The Baptist Boys' Primary School

HOBBIES GALORE

One of my hobbies is reading
I actually find it quite pleasing
I also collect Warhammer
I like Tyranids because they're more quick and sly
Than any other army alive

I get a thrill whenever I skateboard
But I actually am quite worried
That I will be desperately hurried
To ward 7 in the hospital
After trying to land an impossible

I like to play ice hockey
Even if my dad thinks it's a load of malarkey
I often play it on the street
I'm usually out on them once a week

I really love to play rugby
Even if they shove me and tug me
And in the art of karate
We defend ourselves with the most cunning of strategy.

Davin Clarke (11)
St John The Baptist Boys' Primary School

FEAR

My fear is Mr Mistoffili and broccoli
Dogs and flying logs
Cats and massive rats
The hiss of a bus
And getting lost in a fuss
My bike going rusty
My eyes getting dusty.

Jackson McGreevy (8)
St John The Baptist Boys' Primary School

My Bedroom

My bedroom is the place I like
To play when I'm not on my bike
It's a place where I can call my own
I only wish I had a phone

It's where I play my PS2
2 player games for me and you
I lay in bed and watch the telly
After my mum has filled my belly

But best of all
When I am tired
I can crawl under the covers
And just retire.

Michael Duffin (9)
St John The Baptist Boys' Primary School

The Back Garden Of My House

The back garden of my house
Is as big as a football pitch
Looks like it's been hit by an A-bomb
With more craters than the moon

My back garden looks like nuclear winter
Or a mine field from World War II
Well, it's not our fault
It's only a garden

But I'll tell that salesman soon
To hit himself with a spoon
The fat old prune
For selling us the surface of the moon.

Michael Maxwell (9)
St John The Baptist Boys' Primary School

MY FAVOURITE THINGS

My favourite thing is football
I play against the wall,
But then I chase my sister
Because she has taken my ball.
If my dreams come true
I'd love to play for Man United,
If I was half as good as Beckham,
I would be so very excited.
Running up and down the pitch
Sometimes makes me sweat
But it all becomes worth it
When the ball hits the back of the net.

Ryan McBride (8)
St John The Baptist Boys' Primary School

MY DOG, MAC

My daddy went to Markethill to get us a surprise,
He brought home a puppy, black and white with blue eyes,
Mac is his name and playing with a ball is his favourite game.

When I come home from school,
He is always waiting for me at the door
And when he is up on the sofa, I say, 'Mac get down on the floor.'
When we are walking him in the park,
If he sees a dog he starts to bark.

Mac always wrecks his bed using his teeth and claws
And when he is out in the backyard, we always have to clean his paws.
He lies on his back and I tickle his belly
And I love it when we snuggle up and watch the telly.

Paul McCann (8)
St John The Baptist Boys' Primary School

MY HOUSE

My house is . . .
Squashed in the middle of the street
Brown door with double glazed windows
With patterns
Inside it's luscious and relaxing
Full of brothers and sisters
Singing
Drying hair
Fighting
Playing PlayStation
Watching television
All of that until Mum says, 'Bed, Gary.'
Brush my teeth
Watch TV
Go to sleep
Everyone consuming, the house stops
Safe in my house.

Gary Crossan (9)
St John The Baptist Boys' Primary School

A FROSTY WINTER

In the winter trees are bare,
The grass is as white as a rabbit's hair,
But as we watch the grass so white,
Some watch some drivers crash and fight,
Our cheeks so red, our cheeks so bright,
It is much too cold to go out tonight,
White and steamy the dragon's breath,
Pneumonia will attack us to our death,
Puddles are beginning to really freeze,
As we feel the strong and frosty breeze.

Peter Forde (10)
St John The Baptist Boys' Primary School

MY HOUSE

My house is . . .
Lonely standing on its own
Bricks of red
Big, strong door
With creamy curtains
I'm number 32
Inside it's bitter and nippy
One brother and sister
Quiet nearly all the time
No grill over windows
My mum hardly ever shouts
Reading in bed, I'm quiet
When I fall asleep
I'm even quieter . . .

Brendan Clarke (9)
St John The Baptist Boys' Primary School

MY HOUSE

My house is . . .
At the top of a street
A big, strong, brown door
Inside it is very comfortable
It is full of brothers and sisters
They are laughing and shouting
Until Mum cries
Then my mum would shout, 'Get into bed, now'
Washed and tired
Then I would fall asleep
Safely
In my house
Fast asleep.

Brendan McCann (9)
St John The Baptist Boys' Primary School

MY HOUSE

My house is . . .
Joined to another house
Big, brown door
With lots of separate windows
It's luxurious inside
Full of one brother, one sister
A mum and a dad
We fight
We shout
We play loudly until
'Be quiet or you'll go to bed!'
My mum says that so that we will be quiet
But when my mum and dad are fighting
I'm like my mum saying
'Stop it, please!'

Ryan Clarke (9)
St John The Baptist Boys' Primary School

FLORIDA

Florida, Florida, a wonderful place
With flowers and hummingbirds swinging in your face
The smell of the flowers
Will give you great power
When you go to the beach
You can hear the seagulls screech
But when it's time to go
You'll want to say no
But home you must go
To the cold and the snow.

Gavin Savage (9)
St John The Baptist Boys' Primary School

A Winter Poem

Grass is like a green paintbrush with white paint on top
Robin's birdbath is no more
And *slam, slam, slam* goes every door
School is out *hip hip hooray*
Now we have today to play
Santa's coming, *yippee, yippee*
Up goes the tree
But *don't* forget to wait for me
It's time for bed, night all
Now it's morning, *yippee* let's see what Santa left for me
Oh *my goodness*, a white Christmas
That'll do me
Merry Christmas, *hee, hee, hee.*

Kurtis McGreevy (10)
St John The Baptist Boys' Primary School

Chocolate

Chocolate is my favourite thing
I eat it all the time
I eat it for my breakfast
And again for lunch
And even sometimes brunch
In a car, in a plane
I've even ate it on a train
Yes, chocolate is my favourite thing
So come on, if you have some
Give, give, give me a ring.

Luke Boyle (9)
St John The Baptist Boys' Primary School

HOBBS

Small and grey
Smart and bright
My name is Hobbs
I jump so sprite
My neighbour's a cat
Big and fat
When he shows
I fly like a bat
I have a hutch
A garden too
To run around in
Just like you do
I've been in the house
Once or twice
But my own house is warm
I think it's nice.

Luke Clarke (9)
St John The Baptist Boys' Primary School

THE COLD

As the days pass by and new days begin,
At the end of the year winter begins.
As the grass crunches,
Snow becomes ice in little bunches.
When you breathe, it looks like steam,
But the snow on trees looks like ice cream.
While children making slides from ice,
Hibernating are all animals and thankfully mice.

Eoin Morgan (10)
St John The Baptist Boys' Primary School

My House

My house is . . .
Squashed among other houses

My door is big and brown
It has two windows at the sides of the door

One big window on the front of the door
Inside it's relaxing and warm

It's full of brothers and sisters
With the PS2 and the TV turned up like shouting

Then Mum shouts, 'Up to bed'
Washed and tired and weary

I try to fall asleep
Happy in my home.

Christopher McGuigan (9)
St John The Baptist Boys' Primary School

Gnasher

He's a bother
Rips the mail
Wags his tail
Really goes mad
Chases my dad
Sleeps in a box
Runs like a fox
He's my friend
And that's the end.

Aidan Scott (9)
St John The Baptist Boys' Primary School

FISH

Big and small
Golden
Cold-blooded
Brilliant swimmers
Round and round
Joey, Chandler, Ross, Rachel and Phoebe
My friends
My goldfish.

Matthew Mallon (8)
St John The Baptist Boys' Primary School

MISTY

A brilliant little dog
Excited when fed
Loves playing in the rain
Soaks all Mum's towels
Plays with her toys
Dirties in the house
But loved by all.

Stephen Massey (8)
St John The Baptist Boys' Primary School

MY ISLAND

I wish I had an island
No bedtime, no boundaries, no fleas
I wish I had an island
Sunshine, sand and salty seas.

Fintan Monaghan (9)
St John The Baptist Boys' Primary School

SPIDERS

I hate spiders
Creepy and crawly
Always on the walls
Also on the ceiling
People hear my calls
Calls for help
Five times a day
Cry, cry, cry
Help, help, help
My friends laugh
They're not afraid
Are they brave?
I'm not
I'm always afraid.

James Doone (9)
St John The Baptist Boys' Primary School

MY BEYBLADE

It's small and round and fast
You don't know where it goes
It just keeps spinning round and round
It keeps you on your toes
Mine is grey and green in colour
I hold it in my hand
And when I feel like spinning
I pull its yellow band
It's my Beyblade
And it's No.1.

Ryan Reilly (8)
St John The Baptist Boys' Primary School

MY BUDGIE

He lives in a cage
Always in a rage
A nesting box
The size of an ox
Flies high in the sky
When he dies
I will cry
Has a red head
I call him Fred
I give him seeds
That's what he needs
Every night he goes to bed
He went to the toilet once
On my head
Oh Fred
Why on my head?

Sean Doone (9)
St John The Baptist Boys' Primary School

MY ROOM

My room is blue
You'd love it too
With toys and games
Lying all around
There's fun for everyone
My friends as well
A cosy bed
For me at night
Thank you Mum for getting it right.

Emmanuel Watson (9)
St John The Baptist Boys' Primary School

My House

My house is . . .
Squashed in among other houses
Strong, white front door
With big, gold knocker
It is luxurious
3 brothers, no sisters
All roaring
Mum cries, 'Bedtime!'
We brush our teeth
Stomp up the stairs
We sometimes talk
But my mum says, 'Stop talking!
Go to sleep!'
Snore noisily
At 10.30pm
In my safe, comfortable home.

Gareth Booth (9)
St John The Baptist Boys' Primary School

The Cobra And The Mongoose

The mongoose scampers through the grass
He never goes near the cobra's path
The cobra watches with his beady eye
As the little mongoose runs on by

The cobra is hungry, he's looking for food
He searches about his neighbourhood
He spies a mouse and swallows him up
And the little mongoose can't believe his luck.

Adam Martin (8)
St John The Baptist Boys' Primary School

MY HOUSE

My house is . . .
Squashed in-between other houses
Big, strong, brown door with a gold mailbox
Inside it's luxurious, relaxing and soft
Three brothers and one lonely sister
One calm, two nuts and sister - just weird
Then all laughter and shouting consuming the house
After ten minutes Mum comes home and shouts, 'To bed!'
Want to stay up but I fall asleep
On the floor
Dad carries me to bed
Unharmed and safe
In my luxurious, relaxing and soft bed
In my secure house.

Gareth May (9)
St John The Baptist Boys' Primary School

MY ROOM

The only tidy thing that belongs to me is my room,
You don't even need to use a broom.

All my shoes are stacked on the wooden floor,
Right beside the door.

My slippers are beside the bed,
Not outside by the shed.

My school bag hangs on my door,
Not out by the windy seashore.

I've got a Manchester United painting on my wall,
But it doesn't have a picture of a ball.

James Haughey (8)
St John The Baptist Boys' Primary School

WINTER

The ground is white
With snow and ice
The heat from the fire is very nice
Frosty mornings, freezing nose
Shaking from head to toe
Christmas comes, a time of joy
Mary, Joseph, a baby boy
January comes with sleet and snow
I just wish winter would go
Colder and colder, the month goes by
February's here, more snow clouds in the sky
I hate the winter, I wish it was spring
With flowers and leaves and sunny things.

Peárse McKenna (9)
St John The Baptist Boys' Primary School

MAX

A tail so small
And eyes of blue
Teeth so sharp
And fur light-brown
All he does
Is jump up and down
Pointed claws
And silky ears
He's very small
But not for long
He's very cute
But makes a pong
My wee dog.

Eamonn Stitt (9)
St John The Baptist Boys' Primary School

THE DAY MY DREAM CAME TRUE

The day started at seven o'clock in the morning
My daddy got me up, my mummy was still snoring
Into the shower, hair washed, body spray on
My mummy had pressed my tracksuit
And the Antrim top I was going to put on
My first time playing in Croke Park
My nerves had not gone
My daddy, mummy, brother and sister were there to cheer me on
My dream had come true
Playing hurley for Antrim in Croke Park against Galway
But this time things were different
I was going to take Antrim all the way
Home on the bus, cup in hand
Home to the sound of St Peter's Brass Band.

Seamus Rooney (9)
St John The Baptist Boys' Primary School

MY HOUSE IS . . .

My house is . . .
Squashed in the corner
Brown, big, strong door
It's comfortable inside
Full of my sisters
Won't stop picking on me
My mummy tells me to go to bed, *now*
I fall asleep safe and sound
In my bed
Very safe and sound
In my house.

James Keenan (9)
St John The Baptist Boys' Primary School

My Dogs

One is tall
One is small
One is young
With a big tongue
The other is frisky
And drinks whisky!
One is fat
And wears a hat
One is lazy
The other eats daisies
One is sad
One is bad
One is rowdy
The other thinks it is cloudy.

Patrick Fitzpatrick (10)
St John The Baptist Boys' Primary School

My Best Friend

My friend is very funny
His nose is very runny
My friend is mad
He is sometimes sad
My friend got an A in the 11-plus
Then he got candyfloss
He is sound
As a pound
He is a bore
That likes to snore
He is skinny
And quite thinny!

Kevin Carey (10)
St John The Baptist Boys' Primary School

THE TRIP TO DISNEYLAND

The plane was outstanding,
I won't say anything about the landing,
I was up in a jolt
And away in a bolt.

The heat was scorching,
As usual my brother was torturing
Dinner was merry
For dessert I had ice cream and sherry

The next day I was on a roller coaster
But the man beside me was a boaster
Later, I was on a water ride
It was called The Ride of Pride

The next day I went to a swimming pool
I was the only one who supported Liverpool
My brother is such a bore
He didn't even go to the door
Later we went on a boat
But I had to wear a coat

Today is the last
The time flew in fast
My mum cried, I sighed
For we were heading home
To our pets and gnomes.

Connor Laverty (11)
St John The Baptist Boys' Primary School

PENCILS

P encils come in all colours, especially grey,
E verybody uses them for work and fun,
N obody likes to lose them,
C hildren should always have them for school,
I 'll always like sharpening them,
L ead is what you will find inside them,
S o I always like to use them, better than a pen.

Anthony Gallagher (10)
St Mary's Star of the Sea School

SPRING AND SUMMER

Every summer and every spring
The little creatures come out to sing
They sing a song for every tree
They hope that everything becomes free

They hope for joy and hope to bring
Every thought and every thing.

Clare Aylward (11)
St Mary's Star of the Sea School

WINTER

W inter is very cold and it snows, it is very icy in the winter
I n winter me and all my friends always have snowball fights
N one of my friends like the ice because they always fall
T rees in winter are white, the same colour as my great granny's hair
E very winter the nights start to get darker
R emember, nothing in winter is as beautiful as me.

Leanne Finlay (9)
St Mary's Star of the Sea School

WRESTLE MANIA

I love wrestling, it's plain to see
I am always watching it on TV
My favourite wrestler is RVD, RVD he is the best
He has big muscles on his chest
I love to watch him fighting in the ring
When I grow up, I hope to be the next best thing.

Kiefer Crandles (9)
St Mary's Star of the Sea School

FIREWORKS

Fireworks whoosh up and down,
Through the night round and round,
Different colours spark out,
Red, green and gold about,
People sleeping in their beds,
With shooting stars in their heads.

Tammy-Lea Menagh (9)
St Mary's Star of the Sea School

HALLOWE'EN

Hallowe'en gives us all a fright,
It's not good to stay out at night!
Ghosts and goblins and witches too,
They all scare you with a
Boo!

Shauneen Quinn (9)
St Mary's Star of the Sea School

CHRISTMAS

Christmas is a lovely day,
With decorations throughout the town,
Christmas trees peer through the window,
With shiny lights and balls like crystal.
Pantomimes we go to see,
Oh Christmas is a dream to me.
Christmas Day is Jesus' birthday,
That's why we celebrate on that day.
A dinner, feast with family and friends,
Have a wonderful Christmas
And a jolly good day!

Maria McAnallen (8)
St Mary's Star of the Sea School

HOMEWORK, OH NO!

I had to write a poem but could not think what to do
I asked my daddy to help me, but he said, 'It's up to you.'

Should I write about cats or dogs or maybe a little mouse?
Would that be good, I don't know, will I write about my house?

This homework is really hard, I haven't got a clue
Could I take tomorrow off and pretend I have the flu!

My dad says do not worry, homework is really fun
But my teacher will be angry if I haven't got mine done!

Rose Kennedy (8)
St Mary's Star of the Sea School

SCHOOL

We go to school every day
And believe me, we do pay,
The teachers are really mean
And on giving lines they are keen.

They hate us and they are nasty,
Some things they do are ghastly,
Sometimes they can be fine,
But they'll always give us lines.

You'd hate to come to our school,
You'd find the teachers are never cool.
The kids here are really great,
Although, the teachers you would really hate.

Michael Kane (11)
St Mary's Star of the Sea School

THE DOGS

There are different kinds of dogs
Some look like frogs
Some sleep like logs
Some bark like hogs

Some are trained, some are not
Some wear jumpers, some wear spots
The odd one has their tails all chopped
But our dog, Louix the pug, has not.

Mark McCrystal (8)
St Mary's Star of the Sea School

Cats

Cats can sleep anywhere,
On your bed or on your chair,
They can sleep on your lap,
Even make themselves a bap.
They can travel on a train
Or walk down the lane.
They like to sit somewhere soft
And like to climb up into the loft.
Cats climb trees up and down,
Round the streets, round and round,
Into bed one by one,
After they've gone, I feel glum.

Áine Thorpe (9)
St Mary's Star of the Sea School

Winter

Winter is a cold time of year,
With the birds singing in the forest watching the deer,
Children can't wait for Christmas so at their presents they peek,
'Can I have a snowball fight?'
There is hardly any light,
So at night,
People use candles or electricity lights,
If you don't wrap up tight,
Jack Frost bites.

Stephanie Bonnar (9)
St Mary's Star of the Sea School

HALLOWE'EN

Hallowe'en can be creepy
The witch's cats are very sneaky
The witch's nose
Has bulging moles
Hallowe'en can be creepy

Hallowe'en can be scary
The monster's feet are very hairy
They hunt all week looking for a piece of meat
Hallowe'en can be scary

Hallowe'en can be fun
You get sweets and run
You trick or treat
Until you have sore feet
Hallowe'en can be fun.

Christopher Taplin (10)
St Mary's Star of the Sea School

FIREWORKS

Fireworks, sparklers, twirlers and vasefire,
Twinkle across the sky,
Twirlers, twirlers,
Watch them go round,
Then they fall and hit the ground.
Red, blue, green and gold,
Sparkling in the sky,
To brighten up the cold.

Caoimhe Cleary (8)
St Mary's Star of the Sea School

SUMMER AND WINTER

In summer all the days are long,
When you wake up, the birds sing their song.
It is quite cheerful when you hear them sing,
It makes you change everything.
When the summer is all gone,
Winter begins to come along.
All the kids have snowball fights,
It is always during the nights.
Everyone slips on ice in winter,
They all look forward to summer again.

Iarlaith Rooney (8)
St Mary's Star of the Sea School

HULLABALOO

Hugs, kisses, cuddles too
You don't need to feel so blue
Love makes the world go round
Look around, it will be found
Before the spring and in the Fall
At the time when you feel sad
Look around, don't feel so bad
Only love can make it right
Oh, try your best with all your might.

Christina Morrison (9)
St Mary's Star of the Sea School

BIRTHDAYS

Birthdays are full of joy
When you run about catching boys
Playing all day long
And people are singing songs

Birthdays are full of joy
You never stop playing with your toys
When your mum's baking a cake
She says, 'For goodness sake!'

If you have a brother or a sister
They always wreck your birthday
They always have to show off
And they always make fun

When your birthday is over
You don't want your friends to go
But soon you feel tired
And go upstairs to bed.

Shirley-Ann Quinn (11)
St Mary's Star of the Sea School

TELL ME LITTLE WOODWORM

Tell me little woodworm
Eating through the wood
Surely all that sawdust
Isn't going to do you any good?

Tell me little woodworm
Where is my chair?
It couldn't disappear into thin air.

Martin McCartney (9)
St Mary's Star of the Sea School

FIREWORKS

Fireworks, fireworks,
Red and gold,
Some are like rainbows,
Some are very bold,
Blazing sparks fly into the sky,
Sometimes I see a dragon's eye,
Purple, blue, orange and green,
Flash! Boom! Bang!
What a
    D
     R
      E
       A
        M!

Stacey Hughes (9)
St Mary's Star of the Sea School

BEST FRIENDS

Best friends are always there and never apart,
Cos we all know they are there from the start.

You can have so much fun with best friends,
Cos when they are there, the fun never ends.

You can always trust your best friend,
Cos when you're with them your friendship never ends.

We are best friends forever
And if people ask us will we break up, we'll say, 'Never!'

Kerry Fegan (10) & Jemma McIlveen (9)
St Mary's Star of the Sea School

WASHING UP

Washing up smells,
Washing up stinks,
This is my opinion,
What do you think?

After dinner I hide away,
Up in my room,
When I hear his footsteps,
All I think is doom.

My dad makes me do it,
Even though I moan,
I scrub and scrub and scrub,
It really makes me groan!

Lorna Hughes (9)
St Mary's Star of the Sea School

CHRISTMAS

C hristmas Day is so surprising,
H urry up, it's time to be rising!
R udolph probably came last night,
I think his nose was shining bright.
S now has fallen, it's been so much fun,
T ime to make a snowball bun.
M y mummy and sister always say,
A ll we want is one more day.
S anta Claus has already been, done his work and gone home to clean.

Terri Rainey (9)
St Mary's Star of the Sea School

My Baby Brother

I have a baby brother
Who was born on Christmas Day
He has a bad heart
So we were all told to pray

He looks very funny
When he sucks his dummy
But when he starts to cry
I give him a kiss goodbye

He gets put into the cot
To have a wee sleep
We all can't wait
Until he is home to keep.

Lauren Ferguson (8)
St Mary's Star of the Sea School

Seasons

In winter when the fields are white,
Sing a song of delight.

In spring when the woods are getting green,
I'll try and tell you what I mean.

In summer when the days are long,
Perhaps you'll understand the song.

In autumn when the leaves are brown,
Take a pen and write it down.

Sorcha Convery (8)
St Mary's Star of the Sea School

My Sister, Katie

My sister Katie has lovely blonde hair
And when she tries to kiss me,
She kisses the air.
I love my sister Katie,
I always call her Slim Shady.
She's the best at messing about
And she always gets away with not tidying her room.
For some reason at night,
She looks at the moon.
I love my sister,
Katie and me,
I'll be with her always,
For she's the only sister for me!

Aine Mulvenna (9)
St Mary's Star of the Sea School

Hullabaloo

H ow noisy this city can be!
U lster buses roaring and zooming.
L orries and trucks beeping angrily.
L ots of people shouting and zooming.
A ll raging people screeching through town.
B othered-looking and stressed out.
A nxious people wanting to sit down.
L aughter instead of shouting,
O h! Now a nice place to be.
O h! Now they are quiet as you can see.

Maeve McIlroy (9)
St Mary's Star of the Sea School

My Puppy

My puppy has a black coat,
She loves to play with her squeezy boat.
She jumps so high that she can reach the sky,
When we have some food she will whinge and cry.
She loves to play with sticks and stones
And after that, she eats some bones.

Her name is Gismo, she is 7 months old
And sometimes she is very bold.
She runs away with my mummy's shoe
And tries to steal her other one too.
But we really do love her so
And we will feed her, care for her and watch her grow.

Stephen Mullan (9)
St Mary's Star of the Sea School

My Puppy

It's funny,
My puppy it knows
Just how I feel.
When I'm happy,
He's very yappy.
When I'm grumpy,
He's very humpy and stays at my heel.
It's funny, my puppy
Knows such a great deal.

Danielle McCormack (9)
St Mary's Star of the Sea School

FRIENDS

What are friends for?
When they knock at your door
'Are you coming to play?'
Is what they say
We play football
Against the school wall
We dirty our knees
Our mum is not pleased
Friends, friends, what are they?
It doesn't matter what they say
Friends are happy, sometimes sad
Sometimes bossy, sometimes mad!

Jamie McLaughlin (8)
St Mary's Star of the Sea School

A POEM TO MY GRANNY

You were the one I could talk to,
The one whom I could depend on,
You were more than just my granny,
You were my best friend,
So please guide me through this Granny
And help me to be strong
And no matter what it throws at me,
Help me to carry on.

Conor McLarnon (10)
St Mary's Star of the Sea School

DON'T BUG ME

Don't talk when I'm angry
Don't talk when I'm sad
Don't talk when I look dangerous
Or I'll be bad!

I mean it, I'll rip your eyes out
I'll make you go mad
I mean you better be quiet
Or I'll be very bad

So if you don't get the picture
You annoying little flea
My request is simple
Just don't bug me!

Adeva McGuinness (10)
St Mary's Star of the Sea School

MY DOG

My little dog is black and white
I love her with all my might
She is young, playful and bright
And I love to cuddle her tight

I take her for her walks
She jumps with delight and tries to talk
On her lead and heading for home
She still wants to run and roam.

Shauna McCavana (8)
St Mary's Star of the Sea School

Yes, It's Christmas

Christmas is here
Just think about
All the glistening parcels under the tree
A Christmas dinner all for me
Ice hanging from the roof
And hearing the sound of Rudolph's hoof
And Christmas lights all flashing low
The gentle fall of the snow
And Jesus Christ is born
And horns are going *beep, beep!*
To pick up people off the street
But they are all so wonderful
Don't forget about the poor, poor people!
So Merry Christmas everybody!

Sarah McCullough (10)
St Mary's Star of the Sea School

A Prayer To God

Thank you God for everything
For bells that ring
And birds that sing
And thank you God for children.

Thank you God for all you've done
Thank you God for Dad and Mum
For insects and bears
And books and for words.

Bronagh McMahon (11)
St Mary's Star of the Sea School

PETS

Pets are big, pets are small,
Pets are tiny, pets are tall.
Hamsters are so small and furry,
Snakes are so long and scary.

Tarantulas have eight
Hairy long legs,
My goldfish are as small
As clothes pegs.

Choose between a cat or a dog,
Maybe a lizard, even a frog,
A selection of pets,
I can't choose which one.

Rabbits eat carrots all day,
Guinea pigs run and play.
Pets are big, pets are small,
I can't choose any,
Because I love them all.

Eamonn Privilege (10)
St Mary's Star of the Sea School

MY DOG

My little dog, her name is Penny
Common sense she has not any
When she is let out the door
Penny bolts for the gate, that's for sure
I have to run and try and catch her
Before she's right out of sight
I hope I see her before day turns to night.

Shannon Davidson (9)
St Mary's Star of the Sea School

PETS

I have always been a dog person
But some people like cats
I have even heard of people
Who keep snakes, spiders and rats.

It's relaxing to sit by a fish tank
Filled with multicoloured tropical fish
We can watch them dart and swim about
As their tails flick about with a swish.

I once heard of a man with a parrot
The most colourful of all birds
But he couldn't bring visitors into his house
Because the parrot liked to say naughty words

But among all the pets there are in the world
Come to my house and you will see
My favourite fluffy dog that can't be replaced
Lies sleeping curled up on my knee.

Christina Toman (11)
St Mary's Star of the Sea School

AUTUMN'S OVER

Autumn's over, there's a chilly breeze,
The leaves have fallen off the trees.
The clouds are thick now in the sky,
So rain is due soon and birds will fly.
Off they go to a warmer land,
To have some fun on the golden sand.
Back at home, I wrap up warm,
Hoping soon snow will come.

Carey Mullan (8)
St Mary's Star of the Sea School

Spring

Bloom, bloom, hi, I'm a golden daffodil,
Standing tall like a lamp post,
Shining my light all over the coast.

Ding, ding, hi, I'm an ocean-blue bluebell ringing my bells,
I'm only beginning and I'm not playing very well.

Kick, kick, hi, I'm a sunburnt kid looking like a beetroot,
Playing football and taking a shot.

Baa, baa, hi, I'm a snowy white lamb like a ball of cotton wool,
Skipping and hopping about like a fool.

Dust, dust, hi, I'm Mrs Spring,
Dusting and cleaning,
While having a dance and a sing!

Aoife Brown (10)
St Mary's Star of the Sea School

Friends

Friends are special people to meet,
They'll be your shelter when there's sleet,
Sometimes you'll argue and you'll fight,
But in the end it will be alright.

Friends will be with you every day
And when you're sick they will stay.
Friends will stay by your side
And they'll never wash away with the tide!

Shauna O'Reilly (9)
St Mary's Star of the Sea School

Summer Holidays

When summer comes about
Kids go out and scream and shout
They eat ice cream
Then they get a brain freeze

Summer is the best
Because nobody's a pest
All you have to do
Is go on holiday for two

On your holiday you can
Go to the beach
Swim in the sea
Lots of fun for you and me

When the summer's over
You find a four-leaf clover
That's all you have to treasure
From the summer weather.

Colleen McGrogan (11)
St Mary's Star of the Sea School

Growing

G rowing quicker every day,
R unning faster as we play,
O utdoors is better than all the rest,
W inning is about being the best,
I get taller,
N obody gets smaller,
G rowing, what a wonderful thing.

Michael McMahon (10)
St Mary's Star of the Sea School

There Once Was A ...

There once was a dog
Who liked to bark
He slept with the light on
'Cause he was afraid of the dark

There once was a cat
Who liked catching mice
He ate them for dinner
And said they were nice

There once was a fish
Who swam round and round
He tipped up his bowl
And fell to the ground

There once was a budgie
Who flew out at night
A cat tried to catch him
And he dropped dead of fright.

Leo Fegan (8)
St Mary's Star of the Sea School

The Seasons Of The Year

In summer the sun is so hot
You think you're in a boiling pot
In spring the birds love to sing
In autumn you can go out
Because there is no snow about
In winter stay indoors
Because the snow pours and pours.

Fearghal Conn (9)
St Mary's Star of the Sea School

FRIENDS

Friends are people who will share
Friends are people who care
Friends are people to talk to
Friends are people who love you
Friends are people who make you laugh
Friends are good to have
Friends who always come to your parties
Friends buy you a box of Smarties
Friends are there, wherever they are living
Friends are people loving and giving
Friends are forever.

Shannen Savage (9)
St Mary's Star of the Sea School

MY FEELINGS

When I laugh and I am nice,
That's when I am happy.

When I'm selfish and disobedient,
That's when I am grumpy.

When I'm helping and kind,
That's when I am helpful.

When I'm sad and scared,
That's when I am all alone.

But the best time I have,
Is when I'm happy and with all my *friends.*

Katie Vinelott (8)
St Michael's Primary School

What Is Red?

What is red? My bike is red,
So is my shed.
What is pink? My drink is pink,
That I like to drink.
What is blue? My glue is blue,
So is my shoe.
What is white? The light is white,
So is my kite.
What is green? Your chair is green,
So is a bean.
What is yellow? My cello is yellow,
I like to say hello.

Emma O'Hara (8)
St Michael's Primary School

My Mum

My mum is always in and out
She is always up and rushing about
I think she looks nice, my sister does too
She likes to get out to her working do
Sometimes my mum can be cross
But at the end of the day, I know she's the boss
My mum works hard, there's no doubt about that
But when she gets on the phone, she loves a long chat.

Claire Le Velly (8)
St Michael's Primary School

HULLABALOO!

'Hullabaloo!'
Said the mouse to the shrew,
'Would you like to come home
For a bowl of my stew?
Your mummy is going,
Your daddy is too,
They said they'd be here
At half-past two.

I met your cousin, Hullabalee,
She said, 'Thank you,
I'll see you at three'.

Said Hullabalee to Hullabillite,
'I'm going to Hullaballo's house tonight.'
And with that, he was gone
Right out of the door,
He said he'd be back just after four.

I'm writing a speech
And a funny one too,
It's all about fish,
The stew and the shrew.

Said Hullabalee to Hullabillite,
'With the speech
You'll find I'll arrive,
Just after five.

The speech is about
A little boy scout,
Who still has to write
A poem of his life,
It's a very strange sight,
His name is the Lord Jesus Christ.'

Julie McElroy (8)
St Michael's Primary School

I Wish

I wish I was an astronaut travelling up in space,
I wish I was an athlete and always come first place.
I wish I was a magician doing lots of tricks,
I wish I was a builder piling up the bricks.
I wish I was a doctor making people well,
I wish I was a storyteller with yarns to tell.
I wish I was a millionaire and had lots of money,
I wish I was a comedian and people found me funny.
I wish I was an adult and could go out at night,
I wish I was a grown-up and think I'm always right.

Joseph Shields (8)
St Michael's Primary School

Winter

Winter is the season I like best
Having snowball fights with my friends
Then Santa comes on Christmas Eve
When we're fast asleep in bed
He fills our stockings with lots of toys
While his reindeer waits ahead
But I can't wait till January comes
The best month of all
That's my birthday, I get more toys
And a party with all my friends.

Ronan Smyth (8)
St Michael's Primary School

WALKING IN A WORLD OF MUSIC

I love to sit by the reeds,
Listening to the music of the breeze.
All the birds, they are singing
And children's voices, they are ringing.
Hear the music, long and slow,
Drifting down from Mexico.
Hear the owl hoot at night,
Under the stars and the moon so bright.
Music, music, long and clear,
Listen, listen, can you hear?

Even the sound of frogs croaking,
Saves the sick man from choking.
The music of the deep blue sea,
Sounds long and clear and fresh and free.
Music, music, long and clear,
Listen, listen, can you hear?

Catriona Acheson (8)
St Michael's Primary School

THE SNOWMAN

Children like to play
On a snowy day,
Wrapped up in a scarf and hat,
To make a snowman very fat.
We roll the snow round and round,
To make it very high above the ground.
We stick the nose, we make the eyes,
Oh goodness, look at our snowman, what a surprise!

Catherine Rocks (8)
St Michael's Primary School

My Dad

Hang up your coat,
Lunchbox in the kitchen,
Change your clothes,
Fold your uniform.

Eat your snack,
Nutella and toast, only once a week,
Homework on the kitchen table,
No TV or *computers* before homework.

Finish your dinner,
Clear the table,
Come dry the dishes
And do them right.

Tidy your room,
Make your bed,
Pick up your toys,
Out of the bathroom.

PJs on - right now,
Up the stairs,
Toilet and teeth,
Off to bed you go.

Into bed now,
Lie down,
Arms in, close eyes,
Off to sleep you go.

. . . Love you.

Claire McPeake (8)
St Michael's Primary School

ANIMALS

Animals, animals all around
Flying high in the sky
And crawling low on the ground

Baby animals like piglets, foals, even kittens too
And the little calves go moo, moo, moo

What noises do animals make?
Lions roar, hiss goes a snake, sheep baa and owls hoot
I wonder if the elephant's trumpet is as loud as my flute?

Do you know what animals eat?
Well lions and tigers munch on meat
I think donkeys graze on grass
Frogs and toads feed on flies
Oh yes they do, I don't tell lies

Animals, animals all around
Flying high in the sky
And crawling low on the ground.

Paula McKay (8)
St Michael's Primary School

MY DINOSAUR

My dinosaur likes to dance,
He can hop and skip and even prance.
My dinosaur likes to jump,
But then he falls and gets a bump.
My dinosaur likes to run
And then he says, 'That was really fun.'
But then I got a nasty bug
And good old dinosaur gave me a hug.

Peter Brennan (7)
St Michael's Primary School

BIG BEN

Big Ben said it's nearly ten,
It's time to put down my pen.
I go upstairs and Mum says, 'Say your prayers.'
I look out the window and see his face.
His hands are moving at a very slow pace.
I call out Big Ben, I call out his name,
It's time for bed, no time for a game.
I look in the cupboard, I look in a box,
But all I find is a pair of old socks.
I look under the duvet, I look under the bed
And there I find my fluffy old ted.
I'm glad to have you here with me,
My very own Big Ben.

Clodagh Coyle (8)
St Michael's Primary School

MY GOLDFISH

My goldfish live in water, in a tank
And for some reason they have never sank
I think it's because of their fins and tail
Fish swimming skills never seem to fail
My goldfish names are Tiny and Spice
I think that they are very nice
But one thing's for sure, they are my friends
Until it comes to the very end!

Emma Martin (8)
St Michael's Primary School

IN SCHOOL

In school my favourite subject is religion,
In the mornings I feed the pigeons.
In school I like to do maths,
Sometimes I do sums in the bath.
In school I like to do art,
I really wish I could draw a cart.
In school there are some things that I don't like,
Not being able to ride my bike.
In school I love the food they make,
I sometimes have an apple for break.
In school what I really like most of all,
Is my teacher, Mrs Owens, she is really tall.

Stephen Loughran (8)
St Michael's Primary School

WHAT IS BLUE?

What is blue? The sky is blue,
Where the clouds float through.
What is peach? The sand is peach,
Lots of sand on the beach.
What is yellow? The sun is yellow,
Where people play the cello.
What is white? The clouds are white,
It's a lovely sight.
What is gold? My ring is gold
And it is very, very old.

Rachel Speak (8)
St Michael's Primary School

MY TEACHER

My teacher is lovely
My teacher is cool
My teacher has a special thing like my family does too
My teacher is great
My teacher is my mate
My teacher is a star
My teacher likes cars.

Christine Gargan (7)
St Michael's Primary School

SNOWY WEATHER

Snowy weather is the greatest thing
The snow falls down on your house like sugar on a bun
The children throw snowballs at other children
Snow is the greatest thing to play in
I really hate it when the snow goes away
Well, goodbye snow.

Ruairí Cumiskey (7)
St Michael's Primary School

THE WITCH

Crash! Bang! Crackle! Dash!
The ingredients fall with a splash,
Frogs' legs, millipedes' eggs,
Tarantulas' tummies, *mix, mix, mix*,
Bubbles and troubles are her tricks,
The Hallowe'en witch is a terrible minx.

Fergus O'Brien (7)
St Michael's Primary School

DIFFERENT DOGS

Dogs can be cute
Short or tall
Dogs can be mean
Nice or small
Dogs can go walking
Cold or hot
Dogs can have fur
Colours or spots
Dogs are all different
Small or not.

Gregory Woods (8)
St Michael's Primary School

WHAT IS LONELINESS?

A traveller,
In a mobile home,
Listening to hurtful words,
Badly abused,
Longing for companionship,
Dreading it getting dark.

An alcoholic,
Stench of stale beer,
Bedraggled clothes,
Without shelter or support,
Craving for a next drink,
Praying tomorrow never comes.

Michael Madden (11)
St Peter's Primary School

The Beetle

Deathly predator,
Camouflaged in green,
Rapid runner,
Reflective shell,
Brittle-winged with jointed limbs,
Night hunter,
Searching for prey.

Emmanuel Barkley (11)
St Peter's Primary School

Face Of Despair

A rejected child struggles to live,
Lying uncomfortably on his mother's lap,
Praying for love and comfort,
Hoping for refuge,
Looking pale,
A glint of sadness in his eyes,
Longing for a family to comfort him.

Megan Doyle (10)
St Peter's Primary School

Face Of Despair

A perplexed child,
Living in a forsaken country,
Crying for food and a safe shelter,
Frightened and unaware of what the future holds,
Hoping that someday he will be free from hunger and pain,
Longing for a normal life.

Gemma Boyle (11)
St Peter's Primary School

COURAGE

Courage is,
A soldier sacrificing his life in war,
Persevering in writing,
Taking racist abuse,
Defending yourself when out-numbered,
Agreeing to a debate,
Willing to confess mistakes,
Protecting a threatened pensioner,
Concealing your fears,
Accepting a certain opportunity,
Willing to fight for your beliefs,
Assisting a disabled person,
Separating a brawl.

Patrick Brennan (11)
St Peter's Primary School

THE LADYBIRD

Colour copier,
Faking danger,
Living on leaves,
Protected body,
Premier eyesight,
Concealing its wings,
Clinging to walls,
Fleeing for safety,
Tickling touch.

Ryan McCormick (11)
St Peter's Primary School

What Is Loneliness?

A prisoner,
In a draughty cell,
Regretting his crime,
Gazing through barred windows,
Deprived of human conversation,
Longing for freedom.

A bully,
Banished to his room,
Despising his parents,
Ignoring his guilt,
Staring at blank walls,
Seeking revenge.

Stacey Hodgkinson (11)
St Peter's Primary School

Miracle Child

A chilly night,
The wind is whistling,
A hungry child lies in a manger,
Surrounded by hay,
His mother gazes upon him,
His father nervously waits for guests,
Kings and shepherds are eager to see him,
Animals try to comfort him,
A host of angels sing over the cradle.

Jesus Christ the Son of God is born.

Brianne Reynolds (11)
St Peter's Primary School

WHAT IS LONELINESS?

A refugee,
Stranded on a broken raft,
Forced to leave his homeland,
Escaping his wretched past,
Hands cupping his face,
Silently imagining his future.

An alcoholic,
Addicted,
Crouched on a doorstep,
Gambling his last penny,
Watching flickering candles,
Wanting to be accepted.

Stacey Barkley (11)
St Peter's Primary School

THE BEE

Pollen sucker,
Rapid flier,
Inserting a throbbing sting,
Camouflaged creature,
Delicate winged,
Threatening insect,
Segmented body,
Attracted to the sun.

Gemma McNerney (10)
St Peter's Primary School

CELEBRATE

Celebrate
The threatening bee
Collecting sweet nectar
From a bed of flowers

Celebrate
The sound of wind chimes
Tingling gently
Near the window ledge

Celebrate
The feeling of sand
Slipping through my fingers
Onto a smooth beach

Celebrate
The tangy blue berries
Freshly plucked
From a newly-grown bush

Celebrate
The first step
Of my little brother
On a still November night.

Megan Ward (10)
St Peter's Primary School